REVIVING THE SPIRIT OF RAMADAN

Beyond Do's & Don'ts

HASRIZAL ABDUL JAMIL
saifulislam.com

AQTAR MOHAMED UMMAR

REVIVING THE SPIRIT OF RAMADAN: Beyond Do's & Don'ts

Published by **Abideen Publishing**
B-15-1 Bangi Gateway, Bandar Baru Bangi, 43650 Selangor

www.abideenbooks.com | abideenbooks@gmail.com | 012-223 4947

First published in June 2017

Publisher: **Abideen Publishing**
Director: **Mohd Ariff Jauhar bin Mohd Iskandar** (012-2234947)
Chief Editor: **Ahmad Shakir bin Salleh** (018-2590677)
Authors: **Hasrizal Abdul Jamil & Aqtar Mohamed Ummar**
Typesetter: **Muhammad Abdul Ghani**
Cover Design: **Muhammad Abdul Ghani**

ISBN 978-967-14441-4-6

Printed by:
Firdaus Press Sdn. Bhd.

Books published by **Abideen Publishing** can be purchased with special discount for education and training purposes. Discounts for sales agents are also offered. For inquiry, please contact us at abideenbooks@gmail.com.

Learning Partner of

Akademi Sinergi Ikhlas
Membina Legasi Berteraskan Wahyu

Contents

Author's Note

It is indeed a lonely battle. Perhaps a slow process to adapt to all the new routines. No more 'Ustaz Hasrizal', no more sermons in the mosque, and no *adhaans* even from the minarets of mosques to signify that is it time to pray. Living in Europe is not something new to me. Six years of living in the UK and Ireland, more than a decade ago, exposed me to many unique experiences, but none like what I am experiencing currently, as a Muslim in Northern Scandinavia, 200 km south of the Arctic Circle.

Halal food is very limited. We eat mainly home cooked food. Performing basic devotional acts like the five daily prayers is challenging enough. In December and January, we had the shortest Zuhr time, as short as 9 minutes, while Fajr prayer commenced when I was in the middle of the second lecture of the the dark and freezing (subzero-temperatures) morning. This new surrounding has really forced me to relook at what I understand about Fiqh in Islam and has given me a new appreciation of the dynamism of the Shariah which serves to help Muslims practise Islam without difficulty, no matter how odd the context they live in.

It is not only about me and my wife but more importantly, our children. They are also dealing with a new environment. Their understanding about Islam and being Muslims is challenged to the core. They are not only questioned by peers from time to time, but our children themselves have many questions to ask.

Rarely do they ask HOW questions these days. There are many books written to answer these questions. Under the Finnish education system, they also receive religious education at school, specifically about Islam. From time to time, HOW questions are answered and modeled in class.

Most of the time, thinking intrinsically about Islam has led them to ask WHY questions. Something beyond HOW, even WHEN and WHAT. The WHY questions require us to understand Islam, beyond do's and don'ts, questions which we do not think about as often as we should. It was the absence of meaning in religious rituals, the dryness of mere fiqh, that gave rise to the magnum opus *Ihya' ulum al-din*, "Revival of Religious Sciences", of the great scholar of Islam, Abu Hamid al-Ghazali (1058 – 1111). It is only by answering WHY questions can our practice of Islam have an effect on our souls, values and hence give meaning to the rituals we perform as religious people.

This small book was written almost a decade ago. It invites the readership to simply think but not think simplistically, how Ramadan in reality is a help from Allah to aid us better ourselves. Ramadan entails fasting, prayer, recitation of the Quran, giving charity and making amendments. Ramadan brings about physical, intellectual, emotional and social benefits stemming from spiritual strength. It is that spiritual strength that links rituals with meanings, and the actions of the servant with the judgment of his Lord.

I wish for my children to read this book in the language of their study and social life. My wife too always reminds herself and me the need to assess from time to time our children's understanding and appreciation of Islam. Thus, the translation of this book is timely, as a fulfillment of that wish and need. This translation, will not merely be a gift from a father to his kids as a learning tool on how to adapt to life in Finland, but it is an endeavor to share the knowledge and experience in the original book with a wider audience.

I wish to thank my friend, Aqtar Mohamed Ummar who kindly offered to translate this book. The friendship and understanding which has developed between us for a long time has been of great value in helping him to translate what I wish to convey in the book. Our history began once upon a time with me speaking and him listening, and as fate would have it, we now work together under one roof in Khalifah Model School Secondary (KMSS), aspiring to provide a good education to future generations. It is hoped that this book marks the beginning to more synergies in the future.

I also wish to thank my friend Ahmad Shakir Salleh and Ariff Jauhar Iskandar from Abideen Books for their great effort and commitment in getting this translated copy published. Your efforts culminating in the publication of this book have helped to convert thoughts and words into a reading material which will help spread knowledge and goodness. May Allah reward us all with goodness in this world and the Hereafter.

Let us revive Ramadan by asking, WHY, so that the answer to that question will help us increase our faith and hope, in being granted good by Allah, as Rasulullah (PBUH) promised:

"Whoever observes fasts during the month of Ramadan out of sincere faith, and hoping to attain Allah's rewards, then all his past sins will be forgiven."

ABU SAIF
Oulu, Finland
1st Ramadan 1438H
27th May 2017

x

Translator's Note

First of all, all praise and thanks are due to Allah, without Whose help this endeavor would not be possible. The original version of this book in Malay is written by a dear teacher of mine, Ustaz Hasrizal Abdul Jamil. It is a collection of articles of various themes related to Ramadan which he has written over a number of years on his webpage, saifulislam.com. The book contains many points of reflection and important questions that we need to ask ourselves before, during and after Ramadan to make the best of this most blessed month.

After reading the book, I felt it should be made available to a wider audience, not just to those who can understand Malay, given the invaluable content within its pages. Thus, with the permission and blessing of Ustaz Hasrizal, I embarked on this endeavor to translate the book into English. It is helpful that we work in the same place and so I was in constant liaison with him throughout the translation process, just to make sure I stayed as loyal as possible to the original meaning of the articles in Malay. I have chosen, with the agreement of Ustaz Hasrizal, not to translate a few articles because of their very specific context which will make it difficult for the readership to understand if they do not live in Malaysia.

I wish to express an immense gratitude to my mother for proof reading and providing suggestions on the best way to translate certain passages. There were times when I was stumped as to how to translate a certain sentence and she would help me out.

Finally, I hope Allah accepts this endeavor to make the invaluable content of this book available to a wider audience. All good in it, is from Allah and then my dear ustaz. Any error is due to my own shortcoming, for there can be no protection from error except by the leave of Allah.

Aqtar Mohamed Ummar
20th April 2016

Introduction:
The Start of the Journey

"Alive, son of Aware…. found God, but did not find religion," that is my short interpretation of the story of a man who lived during the Andalusian era.

His name was Hayy ibn Yaqdhan (literally Alive, son of Aware). He was a young man who found himself alone on an isolated island as a child, and grew up without having met any other person. A bit like the 18th century tale of Robinson Crusoe.

Hayy ibn Yaqdhan never knew what 'religion' was. He grew up learning the laws of nature around him. Learning to imitate the call of animals, learning to communicate with them while obeying the laws of nature kept him safe. Nevertheless, he felt a deep sense of wanting to see the inner meanings of all that was apparent around him. A sense that enabled him to think about the Majestic Force behind the material world he was surrounded by. All of it made no sense unless it was linked to that Majestic Force, he thought.

Hayy continued to study his own life until he became certain that there was no happiness and tranquility save by reflecting and pondering over the Majestic Force, that is God.

Such was Hayy's life.

His initiative to reflect and ponder about 'Allah' through His message in the form of His creation forced Hayy to willingly bow in submission, to fall prostrate to the ground. He truly felt who he really was, which lead him to fall on his face prostrating before Him.

Everything changed however when Hayy was visited for the first time by a man from a 'civilized country'. His name was Absal.

"What type of man is this, living alone, using goose feathers to cover his privates?" a shocked Absal thought to himself when he saw Hayy.

After trying hard to convince Hayy that he had no ulterior or bad motive in coming to the island, Absal and Hayy became good friends.

Even though Absal subscribed to a formal religion, to Hayy it seemed like the way he pondered and connected with God paralleled the religion as practiced by Absal. That said, they both agreed that Hayy's 'religion' was purer than Absal's which seemed to be composed of purely ritualistic acts. Upon this agreement, Absal took Hayy to his civilized country so he could introduce his 'pure religion' to her people.

The tale above is not a historical account of a real event. Hayy ibn Yaqdhan and Absal are two fictional characters. Their tale was written by Ibn Tufayl in Andalusia, to criticize the people of the time using figurative language.

Why the criticism? Let us continue Hayy's journey with Absal...

Hayy was awestruck.

He was shocked to see the people of the civilized country worshipping just like him. Bowing, prostrating….. Everything was so similar!

Hayy did not remain awestruck for long. He immediately sensed that all the actions of the people there were but an illusion. They worshipped with emptiness without any meaning. None understood why he was bowing, why she was prostrating. Thus, their worship left no effect, no trace on their souls.

Their lives revolved around their obsession with the letters of the sacred texts, while they lost the spirit of those texts. Hayy's desire and effort to find an intelligent man who would be able to accept and learn his nameless religion from him were fruitless. Hence, Hayy and Absal decided to leave the 'civilized country' because they realized the people there were nothing more than beings like animals without intellect.

Why?

Like animals…their lives too were governed by rules. In fact, those rules are almost never broken. But animals are not able to understand the purpose of such rules, because they have no intellect. Thus, people who follow rules without using their intellects, are equal to animals.

"They rely completely on copying the advice of the Prophet and religious tradition blindly without any endeavor to understand the meaning of their actions," Hayy concluded.

Ramadan

Ramadan has come again with the cycle of time.

Once upon a time, Ramadan was synonymous with the greatness of the *ummah*. Ramadan recorded our victory in the Battle of Badr and the Conquest of Makkah. Ramadan also followed the entrance of Islam into the land of Andalusia. Ramadan coloured the victory of Salahuddin al-Ayyubi in freeing al-Masjid al-Aqsa from the Crusaders. Ramadan even bore witness to the victory of Saifuddin Qutz in defeating the Moghul army at the plains of 'Ain Jalut.

Such is the link between Ramadan and the victories of the past. Are Muslims and Ramadan still as intimate as they were during those past glories? How was yesterday's Ramadan and how is it today? Is Ramadan still an exercise and process of nurturing godliness, or has it just become a cultural event to celebrate a time of great blessing?

REVIVING THE SPIRIT OF RAMADAN invites Muslims to clarify their vision.

It is not a fiqh manual which discusses core rules and laws.

It is a piece of reminder for us to ponder upon.

A reminder so that Ramadan is experienced with our hearts.

A reminder so it becomes not a month when religion is turned into a seasonal affair with no meaning.

We must fast not without religion and be not religious without God.

"O you who have believed, decreed upon you is fasting as it was decreed upon those before you that you may become righteous." *(Al-Baqarah 2:185)*

Why Ramadan
Seems Ineffective

" **W**hy Ramadan does not seem to be effective?" is the question I was asked to discuss. A simple question, but the answer is complicated.

We all experience this. Despite all the promises of Allah, His encouragement and facility for worship, we often fail to achieve our goal. The distance between our ideal self which we wish to achieve as Shawwal arrives and our true selves is like the distance between the East and the West.

Why?

Allah the Most High has given us a friendly reminder that fasting as a process that generates *taqwa* is a complicated process. The word *La'alla* which is the pivot in His commandment to fast in verse 183 of al-Baqarah suggests a 'perhapsness', implying that not everyone will achieve *taqwa* at the end of Ramadan.

Therefore, do not be lackadaisical. Our efforts to make use of Ramadan must be earnest. The Messenger of Allah (PBUH) warned us that many will gain nothing from the overflowing graces of Ramadan except hunger and thirst. Thus, the imperfect product of *taqwa* after fasting in Ramadan may be due to either a problem of INPUT related to matters of faith and the inner aspects of our being, or a problem of PROCESS related to our knowledge in executing the act of fasting according to the manual intended by Allah.

Input Problem

If the problem of INPUT is tied to *AQEEDAH* (belief in God), this is where we see a strange group of people who fast but do not pray. How can someone fast but abandon a higher pillar of Islam namely prayer? It is not a problem of law or fiqh, but it signifies a serious defect in the *aqeedah* of the one who does this strange thing.

This problem involving a corruption of a Muslim's MINDSET and WORLDVIEW usually translates to fasting for the wrong motive. An example would be fasting only to obtain its health benefits and not as a manifestation of one's submission to God. Such a fast is empty of any educational spirit and functions only to provide material or worldly benefit.

A corrupted value system on the other hand manifests as a lack of zeal or interest in all the graces offered by Allah in Ramadan.

Ramadan is like the 'buy 1 free 10' supermarket discussed in the chapter 'Forget God and Hence Forget One's Self'. If even after the doors of Heaven are opened, the doors of Hell are locked, the devil is chained so its potential to influence man is weakened, rewards are multiplied and a multitude of encouragements are offered, we still do not care about making the most of Ramadan, it means we have no interest in Allah or His offers and could not care less about Heaven or Hell.

Such a person is truly cut off from the mercy of Allah.

Process Problem

An ineffective Ramadan with regards to shaping *taqwa* within ourselves can also arise, apart from a problem of input, due to a handicapped PROCESS. How far is our fasting done in accordance with how Allah and the Prophet (PBUH) taught us to do it? The foundation of this problem is KNOWLEDGE, or rather the lack thereof. One of the greatest specialties of Islam is that every act of worship must be based on knowledge, not mere conjecture or blind following. There must be at least a basic level of understanding which would allow one to fast and carry out the other acts of worship properly.

Learning Should Never Stop

How unfortunate is one who is 40 years old but fasts with the knowledge he learnt at 15 years of age.

Knowledge must always be increased in line with increasing experience, challenges and exposures of all sorts.

If at the age of 15 we studied that a traveler is allowed to break his fast, perhaps at the age of 21 we need to delve into the details of this issue when we board the plane for the first time in Ramadan. The facility that Allah provides us may be clear from a fiqh (legal) point of view, but we may be hindered from using this facility because of a mistaken belief that it will reduce the value of the act of worship, or maybe because it is out of the norm. For example, let's say someone who is travelling to London in September decides to fast and not use the facility given by Allah. He is free to do so. How many hours will he fast?

21 hours!

The same problem may affect women who are pregnant or breastfeeding. They need to study and understand the permissibility of breaking their fast and the consequences of doing that with regards to making up the fasts or paying compensation (fidyah). A Muslim woman who enters the realm of marriage and motherhood must equip herself with the necessary knowledge relevant to her situation. Upon realization that his wife may have many reasons which will excuse her from fasting in Ramadan, a husband should show his support by fasting optionally with the wife when she makes up her fast outside of Ramadan.

Similarly attention must be paid to the issue of replacement fasts *(qada')* and *fidyah*. Purposely delaying making up missed fasts for no valid reason until the following Ramadan is a sin. Not only must one still make up for the fast and pay the *fidyah*, he/she must also repent sincerely and regret his/her carelessness.

The *fidyah* has been paid, fasts have been made up, but is there any guilt over the delay in making up for the missed fasts in Ramadan?

In the first year fasting was legislated (the 2nd year of Hijrah), the Muslims were only allowed to eat and drink between Maghrib and Isha'. After Isha', no eating or drinking was allowed until Maghrib the next day. If anyone fell asleep before Isha', he would still need to fast until Maghrib the next day. This was very burdensome for the companions and thus the ruling was abolished by Allah the Most High.

As a replacement, Islam requires everyone to guard his *sahoor*. *Sahoor* is highly enjoined upon, even if it be just with a glass of water at the end of the night before Fajr. Eating at midnight and then sleeping until Fajr does not bring about the benefit and blessings of *sahoor*. In fact, such an act is synonymized to what the People of the Book used to do, that is, prolonging the length of the fast after it has been shortened by Allah.

Refrain from such an act

The same applies with hastening to break the fast. It is forbidden to emulate the attitude of the People of the Book who used to delay breaking their fast, thereby fasting for longer than what was ordained by Allah. For those who think they might stuck in traffic during rush hour, they should be proactive in preparing some dates or water in the car.

Let there be no fool who says he would not mind breaking his fast by picking his nose if there is no food or water in the car!

It is hoped that with this little reflection, we can together make better evaluations and optimize our Ramadan so we may achieve *TAQWA*.

An Ordinary and Extraordinary Belief

"Verily you shall conquer Constantinople. What a magnificent leader will that leader be, and what a magnificent army will that army be!" *(Hakim, 4.422; Bukhari, Tarikh as-Saghir, 139; I.Hanbal, 4.335)*

That is the promise of Rasulullah (PBUH) which he conveyed to his companions and the whole *ummah*.

I tried to put myself in the shoes of the Companions when they heard this prophecy from the Prophet (PBUH).

"Malaysia will one day become the winner of the World Cup. And we will proudly hold the Cup up high!" said the coach of the Malaysian team to his players.

"What?? Are you for real. Is this even logical?" one player said, baffled.

"Clearly our boss has lost the plot!" said another player who hails from the state of Perak.

"You should look around you before uttering such words which make no sense whatsoever!" said a player from the state of Kedah.

Everyone was in utter disbelief. Malaysia winning the World

Cup? The Cup that before this has only been held by the likes of France, Argentina, Italy and Brazil? Can Malaysia really do it?

Sounds like science fiction.

That is what I think the Companions might have thought when the Prophet (PBUH) told them, that one day, the great city of Constantinople will be in the hands of the Muslims.

Who were the Muslims at the time? How strong were they? How about Constantinople? The prospect of conquering Constantinople would have seemed even more impossible than Malaysia winning the World Cup!

But that is how the Prophet (PBUH) motivated his companions.

An Ordinary Belief

Believing after seeing is an ordinary belief. A belief without any value of faith, like a researcher in a lab, who only believes his own theory after his experiments are successful.

In fact, believing after seeing, if not properly guided can bring forth an ugly materialistic belief like that of the Jews:

".....O Moses, we will never believe you until we see Allāh outright"...." *(Al-Baqarah 2:55)*

An Extraordinary Belief

A belief worthy of praise on the other hand is believing before seeing, and working towards making that belief a reality.

Because the Companions trusted with all their heart the words of the Prophet (PBUH), even a promise as great as the conquering of Constantinople was not difficult to believe. They believed before seeing, and worked hard to achieve and to see what they believed.

We have never seen Paradise, but we believe before seeing and work hard to see and get it.

We have never been punished in Hellfire, but we believe before seeing it and strive to stay away from it.

Can we believe before seeing and are we strong enough to work hard to see what we believe?

Sweetness Before, Sweetness After

Ask any young man who, before marriage, wants to 'see and feel everything' without preparing himself to give a full commitment to the marriage. Is there anything left to appreciate after marriage? Or is there any sweetness left? Marriage becomes a heap of rubbish waiting to be disposed.

If I say, look for happiness by obeying the commands of Allah, and strive to stay away from disobedience to Him, youngsters should ask themselves, do they have the ability to believe before seeing and feeling?

Think, how able are we to have certainty?

Ramadan requires us to have a high level of certainty so we can attain the things which are not yet in front of our eyes. Let us work hard, so we may see those things we believe.

May every Ramadan be filled with endeavors to realize that ONE true certainty. Ameen!

Ramadan: the Month of 'Sharpening the Saw'

Ramadan is a month of 'sharpening the saw', our saws which have become blunt over the course of eleven months.

Therefore, I resolved to reject any additional requests to give talks for night time and after Fajr throughout Ramadan, except for Zuhr.

My brothers in Japan, Makassar and at the Muslim Overseas Camp (MOC) in Jelebu witnessed my sheer tiredness in the month of Sha'aban. There were times, when I had to stop while giving talks just to swallow my saliva and catch a breath (which is among the symptoms of extreme exhaustion).

I also had no time to read and increase my learning materials. Speakers or writers who talk and write more than they read will quickly become bankrupt of ideas. This is a serious matter!

Ancient Scholars

I recall the behaviour of Imam al-Zuhri who left his Hadith studies in Ramadan, so he could focus on reciting the Quran. The same as

Imam Sufyan Ath-Thawri who abandoned all other activities so he could recite the Quran.

These actions are processes of sharpening the saw, which are done as part of our submission to His laws of nature *(Sunnatullah)* as well as His Divine commands *(Shariatullah)* required to achieve steadfastness *(Istiqamah)*.

Let me quote the words of John F. Kennedy, "The time to repair the roof is when the sun is shining!"

"Prepare an umbrella before it rains," our old folk say. Let Ramadan be a month for us to rejuvenate ourselves and replenish our 'supplies' for the coming eleven months.

Surau Al-Naim, Wangsa Maju

Thus, I usually only accept one or two requests, especially from those like my permanent *surau* (small local mosque) namely Surau al-Naim in Seksyen 5, Wangsa Maju.

Uniquely at this surau, during the first two weeks of Ramadan, short talks *(tazkirah)* are held only during the weekends whereas on the second half of Ramadan, *tazkirahs* are held daily. The *tazkirahs* are done upon completion of the *tarawih* and *witr* prayers, or in other words, after the main agenda of the nights of Ramadan are completed. I am comfortable with this style. *Tazkirahs* (which often end up becoming long speeches) should not be done in between prayers like after four *raka'ahs* of *tarawih* or in between the *tarawih* and *witr* prayers.

Tazkirahs arranged as such only can be done if the speakers are disciplined enough to convey their point comprehensively within the short time given. Dragging the talk for a long time can cause the people who have come for worship to become tired and restless, since they have to sit cross-legged for an hour before resuming the remainder of the prayer.

All the best in enlivening the nights of Ramadan!

Musings of First Ramadan

The first day of this Ramadan feels cool and slightly chilly. It has been raining since sunset today, the last evening of Sha'aban.

This sort of weather brings a sense of melancholy when ushering in Ramadan. But there is also a feeling of gratefulness and joy because this Ramadan of 1430/2009, we are six. This is the first Ramadan for Ahmad Muizzudin, our youngest.

The first *Tarawih*

I took Saiful Islam for *tarawih* to Masjid Fatimah al-Zahra' in Taman Kosas. I chose that mosque because of its ample parking space and I was quite sure Saiful Islam would bump into his school friends. At least he would not be too bored if the *tarawih* or *tazkirah* was too long.

"I met Afif, Abi. Can I pray with Afif?" my son asked.

"Of course. But make sure you pray okay. If you wanna talk to one another, speak softly. If not the grandpas will be upset because you will be disturbing others who want to pray. Can you do that?" I advised him a bit.

"Can!"

I joined *tarawih* in the third row, while Saiful Islam prayed with the kids at the back.

This child has already been circumcised. He is seven years old, but I did not want to get a headache explaining and clarifying to the elderly folk the falsity of the widely held belief that 'children break the row'.

After 2 *raka'ats*, I turned around and saw my son praying with his friend. *Alhamdulillah*.

If they had been playing, I would've gone to the back to 'break' their row.

The Blessing of Being a *Ma'mum*

In all honesty, I really appreciate the blessings of being a ma'mum, not being approached by 'fans' (sounds awful doesn't it??) and of sitting cross legged listening to *tazkirahs*. That is why I resolved to move from one masjid to the next this Ramadan on the nights I am not invited to give any *tazkirah*, so I can pray in peace while observing my surrounding, expanding my view from looking at the floor (as would be my view when I am the one giving the *tazkirah*) to looking at the imam or whoever else is giving the *tazkirah*.

Unfortunately, I could not wait for the *tazkirah* at Masjid Fatimah Al-Zahra' that night in Taman Kosas because the speaker arrived late and I had already planned to leave early since Saiful Islam was falling all over the place due to sleepiness.

"What is the matter with you Yop? It's not even 10 o'clock and you are so sleepy already!" Saiful Islam's eyes were only half open by that time.

"I am sleepy..." he said softly.

"Yop, do you know which of Allah's creatures sleeps at 7 o'clock?"

"What is it?"

"Chickens! That is the creature that becomes sleepy and 7 o'clock. Humans should be able to stay awake at least until 9 or 10 o'clock before falling asleep. See, because you love to eat chicken, you are beginning to fall asleep like one too!" I nagged.

"What are you going on about Abi?? I don't even get it!"

I just laughed and let Saiful Islam sleep in the car.

The rain continued to fall, more like a drizzle. I stopped at a shop to buy some dates and bread. So typical of me to do things last minute like this.

The First Night of Ramadan

It was difficult to close my eyes. I was sad thinking about the departure of Ustaz Asri Ibrahim (Rabbani) who certainly would not have known that the last Ramadan would be his last. He and Rabbani had signed a contract for a program at Singgahsana Hotel, and all sorts of preparations had been made to welcome Ramadan, but God called him back at the doorstep of Ramadan.

May Allah shower His mercy upon him, and give him rest in his new abode.

I read some Quran and opened my Fiqh books to revise some things about fasting. As usual, questions about *fidyah* for pregnant and breastfeeding women, *kaffarah* of fasting, the use of inhalers and the like, all need to be revised to refresh the memory in my head.

The clock hands pointed close to one o'clock.

"Tomorrow after *suhoor*, I need to go to Alam Damai for a Fajr talk," I thought to myself.

After thinking and thinking about all the boring matters of this world, I finally fell asleep.

The First Fajr of Ramadan

Honestly, I was quite enthusiastic about giving the talk in Alam Damai because they have invited me so many times, but due a busy schedule, I have not been able to accept their invitations. Finally, this Fajr, I have the opportunity to fulfill their request.

For suhoor, I only had one date and a glass of water. I quickly made my way to Alam Damai. I felt a peace of mind driving on roads which were empty on a tranquil morning. With the aid of my GPS, I finally arrived at Surau at-Taqwa right at the moment the Imam said the takbiratul ihram to begin the prayer. A peculiar feeling crossed my mind, because the surau seemed quiet with very few people praying. It was an end lot house loaned by a rich man to be used as a surau for the people living in Alam Damai.

"Have you arrived ustaz? I don't see you…?" Haji Sabri sent me an SMS.

"I'm here already, in the second row. In Surau at-Taqwa right?" I replied the SMS.

Suddenly, I was jolted into a realization, asking myself hastily, whether the talk that morning was supposed to be at Surau at-Taqwa or the MOSQUE? Only then did I remember reading about a project to build a mosque in Alam Damai on a blog of a friend, Izhar Hadafi. As far as I knew, the mosque was not yet complete.

Subhanallah!!!

I was at the wrong place! The morning *tazkirah* was scheduled not in Surau at-Taqwa, but at the mosque which has been fully operational since the previous week.

I panicked.

Thank God the GPS was quick to locate the destination. Luckily, in just five minutes I arrived at the mosque and the congregation was patiently waiting for me.

I managed to deliver the talk. Congratulations to the people of Alam Damai on their new mosque this Ramadan. I am happy for all of you. Just feeling a little dizzy from the confusion which occurred this peaceful morning.

A Story on the First Day of Ramadan

Reminiscing the Ramadan of 2007:

"Abi, we open (break) our fast this evening right?" Yop (Saiful Islam) asked me.

"Yes, why Yop?" I replied.

"This evening we open our fast. When do we close it then?"

Err, I was dumbfounded for a while. It is quite difficult to respond to kids who have learned words with opposite meanings.

"We close our fast at the end of the fasting month, Yop." I attempted to respond.

"Ooo....," he answered while standing and watching his Abi and Ummi preparing to break their fast.

Ramadan has come again. The previous Ramadan, we were four, this time we are five. This is the first Ramadan for Imad.

Yop is not ready to fast, but my wife and I have begun to make him understand the meaning of fasting. Naurah and Imad on the other hand are just living their lives as usual, eating from our plates when we break our fast.

Reading the Quran

"Don't you think Abi is good at reading the Quran?" I asked Yop and Naurah who have been intently listening to me reciting the first and second juz (portions of the Quran of which there are thirty) since yesterday.

"You're great. You read so fast Abi!" said Yop.

"If you read quickly, then it's fun. If you wish to read quickly Yop, you need to read *Iqra'* always. Don't be lazy," I teased him.

Saiful Islam nodded.

I often await the arrival of Ramadan to increase my 'credit hours' for reading the Quran. There are a few important things in my life that I earnestly anticipate with the coming of Ramadan.

Having dinner with the family, praying together and reciting as much Quran as possible.

These are the three things I look forward to every Ramadan.

That said, when I look at my IIUM (International Islamic University of Malaysia) study timetable, the ever increasing exams, and my wife's work schedule, it would seem that there is going to be little opportunity to do these things. In fact, it is very likely that I will have to pray the *Eid* Prayer in the hospital because my wife will be working on that day. But that is better than celebrating *Eid* in my hometown on the first day, then rushing back to Kuala Lumpur for work on the second day.

A Long Life with Good Actions

Man often asks Allah for a long life, but there is discussion amongst the scholars about the permissibility and benefit of making such a supplication. We often assume that a long life means an increase in the number of days, months and years of our lives. But in the sight of Allah, the way He shortens our lives may be far more unique and subtle.

Allah extends our lives by increasing the quality of our lives, by helping us immerse ourselves in beneficial and valuable works.

Man's life is shortened when he lives a life, even if it may be long, without meaning, without contribution, without a name, one that is completely forgotten upon death.

The *ummah* at the end of times, will be tested with the feeling that the 24 hours gifted to us by Allah in a day runs out too quickly. We forget that this is the same amount of time that was granted to the great generations and scholars before us like Imam Nawawi. We ought to realize that the reason we feel time passes so very quickly is because we busy ourselves with useless matters, and thus we fail to see the effect of time on our lives when we look back at our past.

"How quickly time passes!" we say the moment Ramadan arrives.

It is not time that moves quickly, but it is we who are slow in catching up and using it wisely. May our Ramadan be more meaningful than the one before this, for it may be our last. Ameen.

Between the Moon
and the Sun

"What's so special about fasting in Ramadan and not in September?" I asked.

The participants of the Fiqh of Travellers module were dumbfounded.

Not because they did not know the answer, but because they could not find the link between Ramadan and September.

"Both are the 9th months of the Gregorian and Hijri calendars," said one participant.

"True indeed. But is it the case that Ramadan always occurs in September?" I challenged them further.

"Certainly not. In fact, Ramadan arrives 10 days earlier every year compared to the previous year," the participant responded.

Exactly! That is what I was trying to get across. Every year, Ramadan occurs 10 days earlier than the previous year. Ramadan has coincided with December, and it can coincide with June too.

The wisdom therein is great.

The wisdom is clear for those who have travelled to the north and south of the planet.

When Ramadan coincides with December, it means the Muslims living in the Northern Hemisphere will celebrate this blessed month, in winter. Besides the cold weather, which helps mitigate the feeling of thirst that can sometimes be quite challenging, the days in winter are shorter compared to the nights. Fajr is late, and Maghrib is early.

"How early ustaz?" asked another participant.

"Fajr can be as late as 7.30am and Maghrib as early as 4pm!" I answered.

"Wow, amazing!" the students murmured, awestruck.

"But it is a different story in summer. When Ramadan coincides with July, the opposite happens. The days become long, and the nights short," I explained further.

"Like how long and short?" asked a young boy who was going to depart for America.

"I'm not so sure about America. But where I worked in North Ireland, Fajr can be as early as 2.15am and Maghrib as late as 9.45pm!" I replied.

They were shocked.

"Luckily I'm back in Malaysia. If not, you'd see only bones in front of you," I joked.

They laughed, but their anxiety was palpable. I am staying in Malaysia, and they were going to fly to their respective destinations for study. They will be fasting away from home, in faraway lands, celebrating Ramadan in summer whose days are very long and nights very short.

"But those who will be going to Australia or New Zealand are fortunate. Contrary to the UK, America, Russia and Japan, it is winter during the months of June, July and August," I continued my talk.

That certainly is the case.

If all these years, the Muslims in the Southern Hemisphere, like those living in Australia, New Zeland, South Africa and Argentina were tested with Ramadans that coincided with November, December and January which is summer time for them, the Muslims in the Northern Hemisphere were fasting during winter. Now, when the Muslims in the Northern Hemisphere have to fast long hours because Ramadan falls during summer, those in the Southern Hemisphere on the flipside will have the fortune of fasting shorter and easier days.

Reside wherever one wishes, with Islam, one will taste the justice of Allah the Most Glorious Most High.

Better still, if one stays in Malaysia, from cradle to grave, one will always experience a moderate and equal fast.

This is very different from Christianity which uses the normal Gregorian calendar which is based on the revolution of the Earth around the Sun. The 25th of December will always be cold in the north of the planet, and hot in the south. The image of Christmas in Australia and New Zealand, is never the same as the one celebrated in the UK and America, since it is always winter in December in the north, and summer in the south.

Islam is the religion of the fitrah.

Is it not a beautiful thing?

The Wisdom of Fasting for Husband-Wife Relationships

I have written previously about the strangest story related to me on how easily a married couple decided to end their relationship. Just because of toothpaste, the marriage contract was dissolved.

The cause is lack of self-control. One can read any motivational book, listen to any great talk or anything of that sort, but without self-control, all of that effort is in vain.

I retell this story here because of how relevant it is to the theme of this book.

The True Meaning of Strength

Reflect upon the advice of the Prophet (PBUH):

"The strong man is not the one who wrestles others; rather, the strong man is the one who controls himself at times of anger." *[The Book of Al-Birr: Sahih Muslim]*

A boxing champion will fail to save his marriage if his might lies only in defeating his enemy in the ring, and not in having self-control at a time when anger overwhelms his being.

A CEO may not save his household which comprises of one woman and two teenage kids, even though he is so successful when it comes to managing a company of 500 workers. All because of loss of self-control.

Hence, the Prophet's Sunnah (PBUH) of quoting three verse from the Quran, all relating to *TAQWA*, whenever he gives a short sermon during the solemnization of marriage contracts *(nikah)*.

The Meaning of *Taqwa*

Umar ibn al-Khattab asked Ubay ibn Ka'ab (may Allah be pleased with them) about *TAQWA*, and Ubay responded, "Have you walked on a path full of thorns?" Umar said, "Yes, of course!" Ubay questioned further, "And what did you do?" Umar replied, "I lifted my lower garment and walked carefully." Ubay concluded, "That is *TAQWA*."

How clear is the parable Ubay gave Umar. If *TAQWA* is translated into the context of a household, then it would mean the ability to navigate one's self properly especially when encountering the inevitable thorns and prickles of married life. Stepping cautiously, that is having good self-control.

One wife says, "I hate your attitude of keeping silent. If you are not happy with me anymore…"

Stop!

Do not finish the sentence.

Learn proper self-control. Do not fall prey to the volatile emotion at that point. Do not be too quick to ask to be let go. Do not so easily ask for DIVORCE.

That said, from an angle, if it is the wives who often lose their self-control, it is still understandable since they are creatures filled with feeling. Their emotions are like the oceans. Thus, loss of judgment can easily happen.

Husbands need to be prepared to face a mouth that easily asks for divorce.

However, what about cases where the husbands are equally emotional?

They can be too quick to lose a good sense of judgment, shouting away, either because of the heavy stresses of life, or an ego that is as high as the mountains. Indeed, the manliness of a man is not in the length of his moustache, the hairiness of his body or the deepness of his voice like Sohaimi Mior Hassan. The manliness of a man is in his strength to control himself, in navigating life, especially the sea of married life.

Think far.

Be calm.

Act in a rational way.

Not emotional.

The Wisdom of Ramadan

There is much benefit in the fast of Ramadan with regards to saving our households. The foundation of married life is *TAQWA*, and is it not the case that Ramadan was ordained for that purpose?

"You who have iman! fasting is prescribed for you, as it was prescribed for those before you – so that hopefully you will have *taqwa* –" *(al-Baqarah 2:183)*

So great is Allah's love for us that He has gifted us a month in which we can learn to attain *TAQWA*, our provision for a peaceful marriage and household.

What is it that fasting teaches which increases our *taqwa*?

Not eating because there is no food has no value of learning

Drinking because there is no water is not a type training.

When we have an abundance of food and we choose not to eat in obedience to Allah, that is training. It is a training to say NO to some of our wants, so we can increase our self-control!

That is *TAQWA*, controlling our desires to save ourselves, marriages, wives and children.

Slaves to Our Selves

When a person is not able to say NO to some of his/her wants, it becomes a disaster with great destructive power. Reflect upon the words of Allah:

"Have you seen him who takes his whims and desires to be his god – whom Allah has misguided upon knowledge, sealing up his hearing and his heart and placing a blindfold over his eyes? Who then will guide him after Allah? So will you not pay heed?" *(al-Jathiyah 45:23)*

Believing in a false god is not restricted to worshipping a grave or an idol. When Allah says X, while our *nafs* wants Y and we give preference to what our *nafs* (the self) wants over the command of Allah, then we have made our *nafs* our God. Who are those who fall into this category? They are those who do not have the ability to say NO to the inclinations and demands of their own *nafs*.

When one is not able to control one's self, then one is a slave to himself, prioritizing his desires to the exclusion of everything else.

A person like this, even if he is very knowledgeable cannot do much at all with his knowledge because his decisions are not upon that knowledge but are based on his unrestrained desires.

Professor.

Ustaz.

Thinker.

All of them will fail miserably if their knowledge does not prevent them from obeying their desires which often leads to destruction.

This is where the wisdom of Ramadan can be appreciated. Fasting and everything that goes along with it helps us to learn self-control i.e. being able to say no to ourselves when what we desire brings harm and no benefit.

Calm in the Face of Provocation

Fasting is not just about withholding ourselves from eating and drinking. Truly, fasting is also about staying away from things which are of no benefit and vulgar.

When any one of you gets up in the morning in the state of fasting, he should neither use obscene language nor do any act of ignorance. And if anyone slanders him or quarrels with him, he should say: "I am fasting, I am fasting." *[Sahih Muslim]*

Especially in Ramadan, if we find ourselves trapped in a situation that can lead to us losing our heads from anger, then we should quickly remind ourselves the advice of the Prophet to not respond or argue back. Enough it is as a response to say "I am fasting!"

Not because we want to turn ourselves into victims, but as a learning process towards self-control. This lesson is the greatest art one needs to master to keep things in the house under control.

Do not be like one who responds to nagging with more nagging, to curses with more curses. Actions which cause us to become angry should not be responded with similar actions which perpetuate the cycle of anger. Learn to control yourself, learn to not respond in haste or act on whim.

Hopefully if this wisdom of Ramadan is learnt, there will less fights, less arguments and ultimately less divorces.

Let us save our households with the wisdom of Ramadan and *taqwa*.

The Wisdom of Fasting for Youngsters

Like the previous article "The Wisdom of Fasting in the Relationship between Husband and Wife", this article too is inspired by a story. There was a young man, who was desperate to get married because every day he would see his lover during lectures. Even fasting could not restrain the raging love inside of him.

"I do fast ustaz, but that desire does not seem to fade away! It is quite normal for us students to fast especially at the end of the month. If we have no stock of instant noodles left, then fasting is the last resort!" he explained when I suggested that he should fast as an alternative to his desire to marry.

"That sort of fast does not help you. It is not a type of training. It is not the fast that was meant by the Prophet (PBUH)," I said.

It seems like I have found one of the 'problems' of this child.

"What do you mean, ustaz?" he asked for clarification.

Fasting as a Shield

It was narrated that 'Abdullah said: "The Messenger of Allah said to us: 'O young men, whoever among you can afford it, let him get married, for it is more effective in lowering the gaze and guarding chastity, and whoever cannot then he should fast, for it will be a restraint *(wija')* for him.'" *[Agreed upon]*

That is the advice of the Messenger (PBUH) to youngsters who are desirous, but do not yet have the means to get married.

They are told to fast because fasting acts as a shield that protects them from consuming what has been forbidden by Allah.

However, the mechanism of fasting as a shield needs to be understood properly. If the shield is just a barrier that causes a buildup of desire, then the risk is high. A dam can rupture if the pressure of the water is not monitored and allowed to increase without surveillance.

Not eating because there is no food is not the type of fasting which tames the raging desires of young men.

Not drinking because there is no drink is not the fast which restrains the ever-desirous *nafs*.

On the contrary, if we choose to fast when there is abundance of food and drink because we wish to obey Allah, then the fast functions as a training.

What training is that?

The training to say NO to some of our desires in obedience to Allah. A training that increases our self-control.

Not Just the Fast of Ramadan

This is what must be appreciated by youngsters who choose to fast as a means of restraining themselves whilst waiting for marriage. They must fast while being aware of why they are doing so. Only then will fasting act as a form of training. If fasting merely serves to restrain one's self from raging desires from sunrise to sunset, then it will fail because the *nafs* will rebel with a great rebellion upon nightfall.

Instead fasting should be appreciated as a training to achieve self-control, to say no. This effect can be truly appreciated in the case of optional fasting when everyone else is not fasting. It really is an exercise of saying NO to most of our desires in our endeavor to obey Allah.

The Effect of a Luxurious Life

In our current living situation where everything we want is obtained easily, the strength to control our wants is sacrificed. All that we want we obtain, when the want involves something like books, clothes, gadgets or even holidays. But when the thing we want is marriage, it is not as simple as fulfilling the other wants.

There are many considerations involved.

Thus, the desire of wanting to get married may be the first time a youngster encounters a want that cannot be achieved. However, owing to his lack of will power to say NO and control his desires because he is too used to getting whatever he wants, any wisdom and academic prowess he has becomes void of any value.

Defeated.

People who cannot say no to some of their desires have become slaves to their *nafs* and own selves. Such people have been misguided by Allah, even though they may have much knowledge.

Have you seen him who takes his whims and desires to be his god – whom Allah has misguided upon knowledge, sealing up his hearing and his heart and placing a blindfold over his eyes? Who then will guide him after Allah? So will you not pay heed? *(al-Jathiyah 45:23)*

That is the disaster of weak self-control. One gives in to all his/her desires until he/she is not able to say no when needed.

Therefore, for youngsters who are in the category of *wajib* (obligatory) with regards to marriage, but are hindered by 1001 hindrances, obligate upon yourselves the *jihad* (striving) of controlling your *nafs* and desires.

Place Your Hand Over a Fire

Every time a youngster fasts, he should remember the 'package' given by the Prophet (PBUH):

Fasting is not [abstaining] from eating and drinking only, but also from vain speech and foul language. If one of you is being cursed or annoyed, he should say: "I am fasting, I am fasting." *[Ibn Khuzaimah, Ibn Hibban, and al-Hakim; Sahih al-Targhib 1068]*

Fasting has been given as a shield. It will only function as a training if one abstains from the following:

- Food
- Drink
- Idle and vain matters in life
- Obscene matters or those tied to sexual instinct
- Being reactive when provoked

If fasting while waiting for marriage is done merely in the sense of abstaining from food and drink, then any benefit therefrom will not last. A youngster should also abstain from vain matters in his daily life. He should busy himself with beneficial matters.

A youngster should also guard himself against rafath matters, that is any activity that can lead to sexual stimulation, whether through speech, thoughts or actions.

A youngster too, while fasting, should learn to not be enslaved by his/her emotions. Do not be emotional. Learn to control yourselves and your desires and not to act on impulse or irrationally.

Fasting is a not meant to be a dam that is about to rupture. It is a form of tarbiyah (education) from Allah so you become proactive and learn to make choices after rationally thinking about matters, and not merely on impulse, based on your emotions.

"*Alhamdulillah*, thank you ustaz," the youngster said.

"You're welcome."

"The thing is, what if I understand all that you have said, but have no will power to do it?" he asked an additional question.

"Oh, there's a simple solution to that. Place your hand over a fire!" I dealt a final 'blow'.

"Oh, *he….he*!" he laughed as there was nothing else to ask about.

You work hard and we will pray for you.

Training Kids to Fast

I remember when Saiful Islam, my eldest, starting fasting in 2008.

"Abi, I'm hungry! I'm really hungry!" Saiful Islam begged. His face was full of pity, capable of melting mummy and daddy's hearts.

"What is the time now?" I asked.

"Two o'clock Abi. Please Abi, I'm hungry. I said I'm hungry, I'm hungryyyy!" Saiful Islam continued pleading.

The First Year

The year 2008 was the first year our eldest learned to fast. No compulsion. Just encouragement. The bait was the joy of breaking fast. Not mere pretentious joy, but a joy granted by Allah as a blessing for all those who fast. One of two joys for them.

"…The fasting person has two occasions for joy, one when he breaks his fast because of his breaking it and the other when he meets his Lord because of the reward for his fast." *(Muslim, Ahmad, al-Nasa'ie and Ibn Majah)*

Perhaps, the joy of breaking fast is due to the dishes being more creative and varied. The greater joy however is because people dine together and they eat and drink in a state of absolute hunger and thirst!

Both of us observed Saiful Islam's condition. His lips, his tongue, his level of activity and temperament, all of which are important points to observe in a 6 year old child because fasting for 13 hours at that age can be detrimental to a child's health.

Failure

"*Aik*, why are you feeding Saif?" Ummu Said asked, with a hint of exasperation, the maid who was feeding the young boy.

"He was begging, madam. I felt so sorry for him," said Aminah, our maid who cares much for our kids.

"Hmm, we are training him to fast," Ummu Saif said slightly disappointed because it was almost Asr time.

"You begged the maid, did you?" I asked Saif.

Saiful Islam kept quiet, guilt written all over his face.

Revoking Privilege

Because our son broke his promise, his privilege of following us to the Ramadan Bazar had to be revoked. This matter requires teamwork of the father, the mother and the maid (if one is employed) to be successful. Revoking privilege is a method of disciplining kids.

"Oh no, I wanna come along," Saiful Islam begged again.

"If you had continued fasting, you could've followed. The Ramadan Bazaar is only for people who are fasting. Those not fasting must stay home." I rejected his request.

Saiful Islam looked disappointed.

"Later, you can eat with Abi and Ummi. But you cannot follow us to the Ramadan Bazaar," Ummu Saif said firmly to him.

Indeed, there is no need for two or three punishments for one mistake. It may give a false impression that we are forcing and 'torturing' him.

That day, we all ate together. As usual, Imad became our biggest threat. His excitement for all the food caused him to climb onto the table and sit in the middle of it, becoming our 'main meal'!

Second Attempt

"Did you fast in school today?" I asked Saiful Islam when I picked him up from kindergarten.

"Yup. You know Abi, today a friend named Aman cried, coz he couldn't stand fasting," said Saiful Islam.

"Gossiping is no good, boy. Did you cry?"

"Nope, I didn't," he responded, full of confidence.

Alhamdulillah, today is the second day Saiful Islam is trying to fast. It seems like he will succeed insya Allah. The clock hands point to 5 o'clock. The key to today's success is activity. Because Saiful Islam was in school, he was busied with all sorts of interesting activities until evening.

Khalid ibn Dzakwan narrates that, Rubayyi' daughter of Mu'awwidh ibn 'Afra' said that the Messenger of Allah (PBUH) sent (a person) on the morning of Ashura to the villages of Ansar around Medina (with this message): He who got up in the morning fasting (without eating anything) he should complete his fast..... The Companions said; We henceforth observed fast on it (on the day of 'Ashura) and, God willing, made our children observe that. We went to the mosque and made toys out of wool for them and when anyone felt hungry and wept for food we gave them these toys till it was the time to break the fast." *(Muslim 1136)*

Free time without activity often destroys our great potential. This matter must be remembered until one reaches adolescence, nay, even until old age.

That evening, I took Saiful Islam to the Ramadan Bazaar. He was given the privilege of choosing any type of food. However, as usual, he chose fried noodles and chicken nuggets only, just as I had suspected he would.

I on the other hand bought *sambal tempoyak daun kayu* as an addition to the dishes already prepared at home. I also bought some of my favourite dish, fried *kuay teow*. Ummu Saif chose to buy some *kek batik* for dessert. As for Naurah and Imad, anything goes, but Naurah likes foods with gravy. Vegetable soup, mushroom soup, *pengat pisang*, or any type of porridge with gravy.

"Allahu Akbar! Allahu Akbar!" the *adhaan* for the evening prayer could be heard from the television, signifying the time for breaking fast in Kuala Lumpur and areas with the same time for sunset.

"*Alhamdulillah*, congratulations Saiful Islam!" We all congratulated Saiful Islam because on that day, Friday the 5th of Ramadan 1429, he managed to complete his fast for the first time.

Effective Training

Saiful Islam has now fasted five full days. Sometimes he begs to the point of crawling on the floor, like an invalid, trying to melt our hearts.

"Ummi, I'm hungry. What time are we gonna break our fast?" Saiful Islam demonstrates his begging skills with full of pity.

"If you break your fast now, then you only get to eat cold rice. If you wait until seven o'clock, then you can eat all the delicious food. Which do you prefer?" Ummu Saif played with this thoughts.

"Emm, promise me Ummi that when we break our fast, I can have chicken nuggets, and noodles and orange juice and ice cream with…."

"*Amboi!* (an expression of surprise at another person's extravagance) So much! Do you think you have the stamina to eat all that? Choose only what you can eat," said Ummu Saif.

"Okay, okay. I want chicken nuggets and noodles. Umm wait, better *kuay teow,* like Abi."

"Okay." We agreed to give our commitments on the matter.

The fast of Ramadan is not just about enduring hunger and thirst. It a process that trains us to control our wants and desires, to learn how to make accurate choices, to learn to act and behave according to our needs, not urges. And negative habits of little children like Saiful Islam, who often forces us to fulfill his wants like buying a CD or a toy, seem to be cured with fasting.

He practiced self-control. He learned to be more rational when requesting.

It could be seen clearly, the growth of his patience and ability to deal with rejected requests within the first few days of his fasting in Ramadan.

Giving Choices

"Tomorrow if you feel too tired, you don't have to fast." We gave Saiful Islam a choice.

Because he succeeded in fasting a few days, we allowed ourselves to give him some space to make a choice. There was some worry in case the food and drink he had at night was not enough to relieve the strain of fasting during the day, especially his consumption of water since dehydration can be life threatening!

"It's ok, I insist on fasting!" Saiful Islam said, assertively.

Alhamdulillah, his own decision to fast will be more meaningful.

We hope Saiful Islam's success in fasting will be an encouragement for Naurah and Imad to follow in his footsteps later on.

Truly, Ramadan is full of processes that teach us to be parents who realize the need to communicate with our children. Truly, we learned before we taught, because what you give, you get back!

Thank you Ramadan.

Praises be to You *Ya Rahman*.

Intending Not to Fast?

"**U**staz, I intend not to fast this Ramadan because I need to sit for an exam," said one female student in her email to me.

"It would be impossible for someone with a weak faith like me to fast in Ramadan because the activities during orientation week are too heavy!" said another male student.

"My sexual urges are uncontrollable and I often masturbate even in Ramadan. What is my fate ustaz?" said one student.... nay, said many female students in their emails to me. Yes, female. Not male.

My face often turns red, my ears hot, as I read these emails.

If it is just one person who intends not to fast, then I can easily consider it an isolated case. But in Ramadan, I am often contacted by a number of male and female students, who from the beginning, voice out their intentions TO NOT FAST, because something is going on in their lives, something other than the concern of food or sleep.

Exams!

Orientation week activities!

Working night shifts!

Not Isolated

All the emails I receive under this genre I usually gather and respond without haste. I deliberately wait until after the first week of Ramadan to respond. They are quite a significant number, from all four corners of the planet. Disappointing!

Where did we go wrong?

The feeble will of our kids is very critical. Forget about their enthusiasm for jihad, defending the *ummah*, liberating Palestine and rescuing their own race from destitution.

If I may speculate, perhaps this is one of the reasons why Malaysia has thus far failed to obtain even a single gold medal in the Olympics. This country is giving birth to a race of people with very weak determination despite having high IQ, great technology, excellent facilities, abundant knowledge and much of everything else.

Everything is cutting-edge and advanced, except its people. The prima causa has been forgotten!

Warning!

The act of deliberately not fasting or breaking fast for no valid reason, as we all know, is a MAJOR SIN with a grave threat from Allah and His Messenger (PBUH).

From Abu Umaamah al-Baahili who said: I heard the Messenger of Allah (peace and blessings of Allah be upon him) say: "Whilst I was sleeping two men came to me and took my by the arm and brought me to a cragged mountain. They said, 'Climb up.' I said, 'I cannot.' They said, 'We will make it easy for you.' So I climbed up until I was at the top of the mountain. Then I heard loud voices. I said, 'What are these voices?' They said, 'This is the howling of the people of Hell.' Then I was taken until I saw people hanging by their hamstrings, with the sides of their mouths torn and blood pouring from their mouths.' I said, 'Who are these?' He said, 'These are people who broke their fast before it was time.'" *(Classed as saheeh by al-Albaani in Saheeh Mawaarid al-Zam'aan, no. 1509.)*

My dear brothers and sisters, strengthen yourselves. Do not cause your comfortable lives to become a trial upon your souls! Whether you had difficult lives yesterday, or live easy lives today, ultimately we will all face the SAME DIFFICULT RECKONING on Judgment Day. The SAME HELLFIRE.

I pray we all meet in HEAVEN.

Forget God and Hence Forget One's Self

"**B**uy one get nine free!" a piece of cloth spread as wide as can be, for sale.

Not just a piece of cloth, but everything else too. Everyone seems to be talking about it.

A supermarket has made an amazing, mega offer, that if you buy one item, you get ten.

Not just buy one and get 10, but all the roads to the supermarket have been paved properly. All junctions to the main road have been blocked so drivers on the main road are not disturbed. Moreover, all other shops have been closed too. All of this to ease our journey to make use of that mega offer, buy one get 10.

With all kinds of lucky draws, you might also get more than 10. There is a special day at the end of the mega sale, where you can even get 1000! Yes, a most extreme offer! Only a supermarket that is rich and profitable beyond this world can offer such a package.

Suddenly, you pretend as if nothing is happening. Languishing at home, deafening your ears and blinding your eyes from listening or seeing the excitement of everyone else walking, running and even crawling to that supermarket. As if nothing is happening.

That means, you really have no interest at all in the offer provided. Not even an iota of excitement, as if it has nothing to do with you at all.

Ramadan

The Prophet (PBUH) said, "Whoever reads a letter from the Book of Allah, he will have a reward. And that reward will be multiplied by ten. I am not saying that "Alif, Laam, Meem" is a letter, rather I am saying that "Alif" is a letter, "laam" is a letter and "meem" is a letter." *(Collected by Tirmidhi)*

This reward is for those who recite the Quran outside of Ramadan. What then about those who recite in Ramadan when deeds are multiplied manifold?

And what is more? *Lailatul Qadr* (The Night of Power) as its peak.

"The Night of Power is better than a thousand months." *(Al-Qadr 97:3)*

Not only Allah has promised such a fantastic reward, He has made the roads to obtain that reward very accessible.

Al-Bukhaari (1899) and Muslim (1079) narrated from Abu Hurayrah (may Allah be pleased with him) that the Messenger of Allah (peace and blessings of Allah be upon him) said: "When Ramadan comes, the gates of Paradise are opened, the gates of Hell are closed, and the devils are chained up."

As if nothing is going on....

Suddenly, we act like we don't know, as if nothing is going on. We have no desire to increase our good deeds, no intention to leave bad deeds. Sin, reward, paradise, hell, all are matters that are too boring to pay attention to.

One who does not give a toss about Ramadan, actually does not want anything that God has to offer. He does not care and does not even want to know. Truly, people like this have nothing to do with Allah, High is He above possessing such servants!

"Do not be like those who forgot Allah so He made them forget themselves. Such people are the deviators. The Companions of the Fire and the Companions of the Garden are not the same. It is the Companions of the Garden who are the victors." *(Al-Hasyr 59:19-20)*

Where the Soil is Trodden

"How to solve this problem, ustaz. According to which place should I fast?" a student studying overseas SMSed me.

The same question arises every year, and I too faced the same question every year when I was in the UK and Ireland.

"Follow the decision of your mosque. Your mosque will be your reference point. Your mosque and your local Islamic council…. that would be my priority," I responded to the SMS.

Every time I conduct student preparatory courses with KRIM (a youth club), in the modules "Introduction to the West" and "Fiqh of Travellers", I always emphasize to the students the importance of connecting with their mosques. They should try their best to worship at their local mosque, frequent any programs organized and follow the decision of the mosque in matters like the beginning of Ramadan and Shawwal, as well as the issue of combining prayers (Maghrib and Isha) in the summer.

"But ustaz, this mosque says this, that mosque says that," replied the student.

Sheesh…. Why is it that every Ramadan we have to go through the same problem, year after year?

When I was working in the UK and Ireland (as minister of religion/chaplain), I and the mosque administration always faced this problem. By right, we in the UK and Ireland do not have to argue. For those in the UK, it is best for us to just follow the decision made by the Islamic Cultural Centre in London or more commonly known as Regent Mosque which is accepted as a place where Muslims convene to decide on issues, while those in Ireland can refer to the decision of the Islamic Cultural Centre of Ireland, or more commonly known as Clonskeagh Mosque.

There is no need for us to ask whose masjid is that, or why not this masjid. Almost like the dilemma of which came first, the chicken or the egg. Never ending!

No Sense of Belonging

One of the reasons I reckon contributes to this problem is the weak or completely absent sense of belonging Muslims in the UK and Ireland have to the place they live in. They come to the UK and Ireland not to spread Islam and translate it into a form of *maslahah* (any endeavor that brings benefit) for the local people, but instead they want to plant their own flags in the ground like climbers do at the peak of a mountain.

Thus, one sees a Pakistani Masjid whose Ramadan calendar follows that of Karachi. The Arabic Masjid wants to follow Egypt if they are not Salafi, while those upon the Salafi path want to follow Makkah. *Turk Cami* (Turkish Mosque) on the hand wants to follow Istanbul. They have completely ignored the fact that they all live in the UK or Ireland.

Usually the Malaysians will just follow one of them amid this confusion. But when their community grows big enough, they too have the tendency to show this attitude. This sort of attitude not only causes problems when it comes to determining the beginning of Ramadan or Shawwal, but it affects the *maslahah* of the whole Muslim *ummah*.

Education becomes the biggest victim. Everybody wants to put forth their own curriculum and syllabus, according to their own countries and traditions, following their own methodologies for their children, most of whom are born and bred in the UK or Ireland. And it is highly likely that none of these suggestions will be useful for the students living in the UK or Ireland.

Because I was unhappy about all this, I registered for a Master's in Education program at The Open University (OU), UK, specializing in curriculum. The desire to study this at the time was so I could produce something that would enable the Muslim community to appreciate their own presence in the UK and Ireland, to realize that they are no longer living in Pakistan, Egypt, Saudi Arabia, Turkey, or even Malaysia.

My studies at OU enabled me to become a member of the Islamic Educators' Communication Network (IECN) based in Virginia, America, until now. Even though I've never set foot in America, discussions held daily involving scholars like Dr. Jamal Badawi and others, has helped me greatly in evaluating the achievements of the Muslim community in America compared to the one in Europe.

If in the UK we were still crawling when it came to syllabus construction and foundation development for weekend schools, in America, the discussion revolved around how policies in Islamic schools could encourage the registration of non-Muslim students in their schools. Or how Islamic schools should fulfill the needs of American non-Muslim minorities in certain Islamic schools.

I am sure the Muslim community in America are not a hundred percent free of the problems mentioned above, but they are clearly far ahead in terms of addressing their needs over there.

The American Experience

One of the reasons American Muslims have been able to move forward is their strong sense of belonging to America. They are proud to be American and consider America to be their home which they are obliged to help build.

I sensed this from the participants of the International Civilizational Youth Engagement Program (IYEP), discussions in IECN, as well as our discourse with our lecturer who taught us the subject 'Islam and The West', who himself was born in Bangladesh at the time when it was East Pakistan, and is now an American citizen.

Equally, documentaries on the television and internet helped me to come to the conclusion that the Muslims in America have accepted that country as their own, their home sweet home, hence enabling them to translate Islam into activities, policies and systems befitting the American way of life.

This is what Muslims in Europe must learn, and perhaps those in Australia well. When we are in a foreign land, it is not a crime to feel an attachment to our countries of birth we call home, but that feeling should not cause us to forget our obligation to translate and live Islam according to the context of where we are.

"Follow the mosque, respect the mosque, love the mosque, enliven the mosque and make yourself a part of the mosque and its community," that is all I say to students who ask me about this.

Where the soil is trodden, thence Islam is practiced accordingly.

Even if It May Be for the Sake of Orphans

"Son, buy this honey. This is very good honey," said the old man next to me.

"It's ok uncle, I have unfinished honey at home. It will go to waste if I buy this one," I responded kindly.

"Don't be that way son. This is high quality honey and I'm selling it for orphans. This is the acknowledgement letter." The uncle was slightly coercive.

He showed me JAKIM's halal certificate. I looked at it just for the sake of looking at it, because I did not think the permissibility of honey was so doubtful as to require a halal certificate from JAKIM. But the document about the Orphanage I studied intently. Not sure of its authenticity.

"This honey is alive so it won't get spoilt. It's good for adults and kids," he added. Suddenly he took Imad's milk bottle, opened the top and poured some of the honey into it.

"*Hish*! What nonsense uncle?? Patience, patience... I'm fasting," my heart was filled with anger.

"What is the price of the honey?" I enquired the price just so I could end this irritating drama in the middle of the shopping complex.

"Two bottles for thirty ringgit," he said while packaging the honey bottles.

"No, one is enough. I don't want to waste." I stopped his hand.

"Why not take two, you can give more to the orphans," he answered with full of misplaced confidence.

I was getting angrier by the minute.

While he packaged the honey bottles, he advised my son Saiful Islam to listen to his parents, pray in congregation and be a good son. Saiful Islam did not concentrate on his words as he was still focused on the man's disrespectful behavior of putting some honey into Imad's milk.

I took out a RM50 note to pay for both the bottles.

"I don't have to give you back the balance (RM20) ok. We give it to the orphans!" he said while putting the paper money I handed him into his pocket.

"Uncle!" I lost it.

"Even though you are selling the honey to help orphans, the way you are doing business is wrong!" I raised my voice slightly.

The uncle was taken aback. He nodded and gave me back RM20.

I did not finish what I wanted to say because I quickly hit the PAUSE button. I massaged my chest and said softly, "I am fasting, I am fasting!"

Even if the profits from the sale truly will be used to help orphans, the way he sold his product was very inappropriate. He forced me, put the honey into my son's milk without my permission, and continued to coerce me into buying the honey until I bought it not because I wanted to buy it, or perhaps not even because I wanted to help the orphans, but because I wanted to get rid of him.

Is this a form of *gharar*?

Even though *gharar* (cheating) may not be as significant as usury, it is something that business people should try to avoid as much as possible in trade. Any maneuver taken to reduce the rationality of buyers until they are driven to buy without mutual satisfaction, or until one party suffers a loss, regret or falsehood, is not suitable with the values of Islam, let alone if it is done for the sake of orphans!

"Give me your phone number. I can call you whenever I go to Menglembu," he said after discovering that I am from Ipoh.

"That won't be necessary uncle!" I resisted.

"Just give it to me!" he coerced.

"If I need anything I'll call the number on the honey bottle. Assalamualaikum uncle!" I quickly pulled Imad, Naurah and Saiful Islam to leave the area and worked my way towards Ummu Saif who was not very far from where we were.

"What was all that about?" Ummu Saif asked.

"An exercise in pressing my PAUSE button. *Inni Saa'eem!*" I responded briefly while we walked away.

My Ramadan has been tainted today.

Orphans for Eleven Months

"The program is coming to an end. Has it been fun?" I asked one of the participants. "Yup, it's been fun! You should come more often ustaz," he said. "Just as you feel sad your parents have to leave you here in this orphanage, in the same way my kids too feel sad sometimes when they are left alone at home because I always come here," I tried to make them understand.

They smiled.

"Give our *salams* to your kids, ustaz. So nice to see their photos!" said the very friendly participant. They had pestered me to show them photos of my family stored in my laptop.

"*Insha-Allah*. So, it will be Ramadan very soon. Aren't you all excited?" I continued the conversation.

"Excited and not so excited," one of them responded.

"How is that?" I was interested to know more.

"It is exciting because during the fasting month there will be many functions and invitations to hotels, and beautiful offices!" he said.

The Excitement of Orphans

Ramadan indeed is a busy month for many orphanages. Their Ramadan schedule can sometimes be full from the beginning of Rajab. Corporate companies of all sorts and wealthy folk come forward to give a helping hand during Ramadan by having *iftar* functions for orphans. Not just corporate bodies, even artists join the bandwagon.

Sometimes, I feel sorry for the kids because they have such a busy schedule in Ramadan, being chauffeured around from one function to another, they don't even have time to recite Quran.

"We suffer because our bellies become too full, ustaz!" said one of the orphans in my motivational program, drawing laughter from the others.

The Sadness of Orphans

If one is tactful at digging deeper, then one would be able to obtain all sorts of stories from these orphaned kids. They are kids who keep most of their life stories to themselves, because often they have little trust of outsiders, but if that trust is gained, then they have much to tell, not infrequently with tears.

Surely amidst all the excitement of accepting invitations throughout Ramadan, there will be some sadness for which there is no cure. Is it possible for them to enjoy all the delicious food while thinking about their mothers or fathers back home in the villages, who may be eating plain rice for *iftar*, or indeed, no rice at all? Surely that sadness will be felt, for Ramadan is a time when families dine together, a blessing they have lost.

"Is that what you mean when you say you're not so excited during Ramadan?"

"It's not that ustaz. That I understand. I cannot do anything because that is Allah's test for me as an orphan," he said masterfully arranging his words. I became quiet for a moment.

"The reason we're not so excited about Ramadan is because we have 'parents' for 1 month, and are left as orphans for the remaining eleven months!" concluded the young boy in front of me. Allah…..

Islam and Purpose

Truly, Islam is a religion that teaches us to have an acute sense of purpose. It is a religion that teaches us to live purposefully. To ignore purpose means to lose meaning in our actions, and hence any wisdom or benefit therefrom.

Ramadan is a month of training.

All worship therein is not just to fill in our time because it is a season of worship, but to produce and stabilize our momentum for the following months. Ramadan is a motivational course, it also a skills course, and it too is a rejuvenation course, so our *Iman* and bodies remain active. Thus everything we do in Ramadan should not be just for a promised reward, but also to help us stop our bad habits and replace them with good ones.

The best of charity is the charity of Ramadan. The best of goodness, is to provide food to those fasting when they break their fast.

Is it just a matter of reward? I insist on seeing it as a form of training.

Therefore, Ramadan is a month that trains us to be aware of those who are in difficult circumstances, orphans, single mothers, new Muslims and anyone who is in need of help. What then is the point of corporate bodies using Ramadan to fulfill their corporate social responsibility (CSR) until the orphans suffer from excessive fullness, while ignoring them completely for the rest of the year?

If we wish to speak about reward, then I feel that if this situation is allowed to persist, perhaps helping orphans in Sha'ban, Safar or even Rabiulawal would be more rewarded than donations by the rich in Ramadan. Providing food during *iftar* functions has devolved from welfare and worship to mere tradition. A tradition that is empty of any purpose!

Everyone is doing it, so should we, but when the orphans are really in need, they are left all alone.

Religions function to train us to live LIVES OF MEANING. When we ignore the matter of being PURPOSEFUL IN OUR ACTIONS, then religion becomes an entertainment and a set of actions that play a joke on our humanity.

Orphans for 11 months, how terrible indeed is your fate dear children!

Ramadan Mends the Tendency for Explosive Retaliation

"I think the turban restricts thinking. It makes people parochial!" said a man.

"You're Muslims, damn you must be from the Osama Fan Club!" said a 'mat salleh' (white person) with full of arrogance.

"Oi, stupid! How many times do I have to call you?? Get your ass here now!" a senior student shouted at his junior.

It is impossible for one's ear not to feel a sharp pain hearing comments like that. One feels enraged, and has all the motivation to react explosively, either by hurling more insults or even by folding one's sleeves to deliver a punch on the face of the one who started it!

However, especially in Ramadan, the Prophet (PBUH) taught us the opposite. I state again his advice:

Fasting is not [abstaining] from eating and drinking only, but also from vain speech and foul language. If one of you is being cursed or annoyed, he should say: "I am fasting, I am fasting." *[Ibn Khuzaimah, Ibn Hibban, and al-Hakim; Sahih al-Targhib 1068]*

If you are insulted, then do not respond with more insults. If you are provoked into a brawl, do not respond. If you are called stupid or even assumed to be stupid, do not be hasty in proving otherwise.

Instead, just say, 'I AM FASTING'.

What is this? Why did the Messenger (PBUH) teach us this? Does Islam ask us to let ourselves be victimized? Should a man force himself to become a Muslim who is not 'manly' by saying 'I AM FASTING'?

Our Manliness

Yes, this is our perception. That manliness lies in emitting an aura of 'Don't you dare provoke me!', or 'Do not disturb a sleeping tiger'. That is our measure of manliness.

But the greatness of the Prophet (PBUH) is not like that. His life story is different.

When a man came to him (PBUH) to ask permission to commit fornication, do you not think the Prophet (PBUH) would have been enraged at such an uncivilized request?

When a Bedouin came to the mosque as an ill-mannered guest who pissed on the walls of the house of God, do you not think the Prophet (PBUH) would have been so angry at his behavior?

Not being able to get angry is cowardice, passive like one who could not care less. Let it be, just let it be. Passive!

The Prophet (PBUH) did not get angry not because he could not get angry. He was actually a very expressive person. His sermons sometimes caused his eyes to turn red because of how much he meant what he was saying.

The Prophet (PBUH) was strong…. With a true a strength, that is in being able to control his anger.

The companions were flabbergasted and wanted to beat up the Bedouin, but he stopped them.

"Let him finish his matter!" he said calmly.

Then he (PBUH) asked for some water and he himself washed the area.

That is true strength.

Strength does not lie in the strength to fight, but strength lies in the ability to control one's self in a state of anger!

We measure manliness and greatness in fighting, by how good we are at explosive outbursts due to rage. But the Prophet (PBUH) taught us that strength is in the ability to control one's self, especially in times of anger.

Do not be pessimistic. Covey (the author of the best-seller the Seven Habits of Highly Effective People) calls it being proactive.

This is the training of fasting. Ramadan comes with a training package that teaches us self-control.

The Training of Ramadan

Do not fast because there is no food, but fast because we want to learn self-control. Not eating in the presence of food, for the sake of God. We restrain ourselves from responding not because of weakness or cowardice but because of we want to learn to deliberate over our actions and make proper choices.

Anger is needed, definitely it is needed sometimes. But if we are always angry to the point that every word we utter is filled with rage and disagreement.... That is not in line with the prophetic example.

The Messenger (PBUH) did get angry, but his anger was relieved through discussion with his companions to determine the best course of action. Anger is an emotion, and when we are emotional we are not rational. Acting irrationally is the thing that often brings regret:

"O you who believe! If an evil-doer comes to you with a report, look carefully into it, lest you harm a people in ignorance, then be sorry for what you have done." *(Al-Hujurat 49:6)*

How to investigate and act correctly if one is emotional and impulsive, always responding to news and rumours without investigation?

That is what Ramadan endeavors to teach. It teaches a Muslim to come back to his senses and get a hold of himself, not to be easily provoked, not to act hastily. This is especially important for *da'ies* who strive for Islam. Our job is not solely to forbid evil, but also to try and change the situation. Have we not been advised, "If any one you sees evil, then change it with your hands...."

What is expected of us is not just to voice out our disagreement and opposition, but to strive to change things. The *seerah* (life of the Prophet (PBUH)) teaches us that very rarely indeed can change come about if we only know how to be angry and blame others.

The Lesson of Hudaibiyyah

Just look at the conduct of the Makkans in the Treaty of Hudaibiyyah. Who would not be mad at their requests? Their requests clearly mounted to a win-lose situation.

"If a Makkan flees to Madinah, he must be returned to Makkah. If a Madinese comes to Makkah, he does not have to be returned to Madinah...." the Makkans requested with arrogance. Ear burning!

"How can you write 'Messenger of Allah'. If you write it that way, it means we acknowledge you and have to follow you. Write instead "Muhammad ibn Abdullah', that would do!" How egoistic they were in front of the Messenger (PBUH).

The Messenger (PBUH) had every right to be defensive. The title 'Messenger of Allah' is not a gift from a sultan or any Arabian King. It is a bestowal from Allah the Most High. There is no reason not to be firm in defending it.

Let us put ourselves in the shoes of the Companions who were present at the treaty.... Will we not be angry?

However, the Prophet's wisdom and strength in not giving in to anger due to the derogatory conduct of the Makkans, allowed him to think rationally with great far-sightedness which enabled him to distinguish between substance and form. The Treaty of Hudaibiyyah offered the most important thing in any *da'wah*, that is an arms truce. He agreed to the treaty despite its unfairness for the sake of preserving harmony. And he used that opportune moment of peace and harmony to propagate the message of Islam not just around Makkah and Madinah, but to neighbouring empires and kingdoms. His *da'wah* became much more effective because of the peaceful truce. The peace treaty was achieved as a result of the Prophet (PBUH) prioritizing substance over form.

A Rude Youngster

Once, a young man came to the Prophet (PBUH) to ask permission to commit fornication *(Zina)*.

The evil consequences of fornication are not too difficult to comprehend. The Prophet (PBUH) would have had every reason to be enraged at his audacity. In fact, the narrations tell us that the people in the vicinity rebuked him severely for his audacity in asking permission from the Prophet (PBUH) to commit *Zina*, by saying '*Mah! Mah!*' which is a very harsh way to express anger. But the Prophet (PBUH) was a man full of wisdom who knew how to respond with the right reaction according to the need of the moment. He instead taught the young man what we call today The Golden Rule, that is, treat others as you would like to be treated.

Imam Ahmad narrates the full hadith from Abu Umaamah *(21708)*: A young man came to the Prophet (peace and blessings of Allah be upon him) and said, "O Messenger of Allah, give me permission to commit *zina*." The people turned to him to rebuke him, saying, "*Shh, shh.*" (The Prophet (peace and blessings of Allah be upon him)) said, "Come here." So he came close to him and he told him to sit down. He said, "Would you like that for your mother?" He said, "No, by Allah, may I be sacrificed for you." He said, "Nor do people like it for their mothers." He said, "Would you like it for your daughter?" He said, "No, by Allah, may I be sacrificed for you." He said, "Nor do people like it for their daughters." He said, "Would you like it for your sister?" He said, "No, by Allah, may I be sacrificed for you." He said, "Nor do people like it for their sisters." He said, "Would you like it for your paternal aunt?" He said, "No, by Allah, may I be sacrificed for you." He said, "Nor do people like it for their paternal aunts." He said, "Would you like it for your maternal aunt?" He said, "No, by Allah, may I be sacrificed for you." He said, "Nor do people like it for their maternal aunts." Then he placed his hand on him and said, "O Allah, forgive his sin, purify his heart, and guard his chastity."

If this young man received a response in the form of a slap across the face in the name of *da'wah*, what good would that have brought?

Self-control, restraining one's self during anger and translating reaction into a more empathic form of *da'wah*, are of great benefit in turning an evil act into an opportunity for good.

This is what we need to emulate. Great victories can be achieved from being victorious in this very basic matter, which is being able to control one's self, to be pro-active and not reactive. Da'ies need to really internalize and appreciate this message. The language of *da'wah* has to be explanatory and inclusive, persuasive and not repulsive, merciful and not wrathful.

The language in talks, newspapers, magazines, *da'wah*.... Ramadan teaches us to convey what we want to say in a language that is full of wisdom and controlled.

It seems that manliness in Islam is more subtle and powerful than what is commonly thought.

Control yourself, and you shall be that Hercules!

Who Is Behind the Quran?

"The Quran is this, the Quran is that, the Quran bla bla bla...." people keep talking about the Quran non-stop!

Everyone seems to be talking about the Quran. Even the far right Dutch politician, Geert Wilders has something to say about it. His words became a fitnah to the world, a fitting description for his film, Fitna, which outraged Muslims around the globe once upon a time.

Many parties want to critique, slam, defend and vindicate the Quran, but they all almost always miss an important process. A process that is agreed upon by anyone and everyone who speaks rationally, with a sound mind, regardless of religion.

The process I am referring to is the process of analyzing the authenticity of the Quran. It is an important step in our *tilaawah* (recitation), *tadabbur* (reflection) and *tafakkur* (pondering) of the Quran when we engage with it in Ramadan.

In the discipline of history, a branch of social science, before any material is used as a source of reference, analysis of its authenticity and verity must be done first. For example, is a shilling, when discovered, original and authentic, or fake? Is the text of a luminary, really the original text written by him or was it written by someone else?

Upon the same principle, the process of analyzing and filtering scripts requires at least three different copies of that script so they can be compared with one another and have their authenticity examined.

The point here then is, before debating about or critiquing the Quran, one first has to ascertain through rigorous study whether the Quran is authentic and true, or false and fabricated.

A Map-Book

"Hmm, I need to get the London A-Z booklet, so I don't get lost," Ahmad murmured to himself when he arrived at Heathrow International Airport. This is the first time he has set foot in London.

Ahmad makes his way to the bookstore to look for a map which will help him navigate the streets of London.

"Hmm…. Printed in Bangalore!" Ahmad was shocked.

The beautiful, comprehensive and cheap map in his hands was printed in Bangalore. A map of London printed in India!

"What?? Printed in 1985!" said Ahmad even more flabbergasted.

A map of London, printed in India, in 1985!

Will Ahmad purchase this map as a guide so he does not get lost in London? Of course not. Ahmad is in doubt as to the authenticity of the map, and will not take it even if it is given for free. Indeed, we would never take something doubtful as a guide.

The Quran

Now let's look at the Quran. It was 'sent down' in Saudi Arabia.

Masya Allah. Can the Quran understand the problems in Europe or Malaysia??

And it was 'sent down' not in 1985, but more than 1430 years ago!

Allahu Akbar! Is the Quran capable of understanding the predicaments of man in modern times, whereas it was revealed more than 1430 years ago?

How convinced are we of the authenticity of the Quran?

"Alif, Lām, Meem. This is the Book about which there is no doubt, a guidance for those conscious of Allāh." *(Al-Baqarah 2:1-2)*

The Quran introduces itself as a guidance, for people who are conscious of Allah. But the main attribute that allows it to function as a guidance, is that it is unaffected by doubt. There is no doubt in it. Thus it is incumbent upon those who wish to approach it, whether they be those who do not believe or have not believed in it, or even if they be Muslims who claim to follow it, to decide first how certain they are of the authenticity of the Quran.

If a non-Muslim wants to dispute the Quran, speak about the Quran, believe in it or reject it, has he first examined the Quran? If you reject the Quran, what is your reason? If you wish to believe it, on what grounds do you make that choice?

Therefore, we must believe in the Quran because we made the conscious choice to do so, not because we have inherited it like any tradition. The question is, how are we supposed to ascertain the authenticity of the Quran?

Language

There are many ways to test the Quran. Is it truly the word of God, the word of man, or what is it?

Perhaps, the first thing we can look at is the language aspect of the Quran. For those who have studied Arabic, try looking at our essays when we were in high school, or maybe just a few years ago.

"Hadzihi madrasati. Madrasati kabiratun, waasia'tun, mulawwanatun, jamilatun, mahbubatun….."

Congratulations, you managed to get an A with that level of Arabic. Sometimes one feels embarrassed reading one's own essays. How low was the quality of Arabic at that time compared to how it is now years later. It's the same with other languages too.

Now look at the Quran. Are we capable, from a linguistic point of view, of differentiating the verses revealed in the 1st year of Prophethood compared to those in the 23rd year? Can we see any linguistic difference between إِذَاجَآءَنَصۡرُٱللَّهِ وَٱلۡفَتۡحُ and ٱقۡرَأۡ بِٱسۡمِ رَبِّكَ ٱلَّذِی خَلَقَ ?

The language of the Quran is remarkably consistent. Once cannot delineate between 'young' and 'mature', with regards to the linguistic style of the Quran in its 23 years of revelation.

Clearly, the consistency of the Quran is something which is impossible for any human being to achieve. No human being can demonstrate such consistency in language like the Quran does.

If man cannot speak with such eloquence and consistency like the Quran does, then it is daft to attribute the Quran to any man. This is regardless of how great one's expertise of language is, because the consistency of the Quran is beyond the capability of any man. Indeed it is the speech of God. The person speaking in the Quran is not a man. It is not Muhammad. Without a shadow of a doubt, the One who is speaking in the Quran is none other than God Himself. Allah, Most Glorious Most High, the Speaker of Commandments.

But of course, if one wishes to study the authenticity of the Quran from this aspect, one needs to have mastery of the Arabic language.

Asbab Nuzul (Reasons for Reveleation)

When Aishah (*radiyallahu 'anha* i.e. May God be pleased with her) was accused by the hypocrites of committing adultery, the Prophet Muhammad and the whole community of believers felt straitened and anxious. How shrewdly the hypocrites slandered and gossiped about *Ummu al-Mu'mineen* (the mother of the believers) at the time, without an iota of shame, undeterred. The absence of revelation for a period of time to defend our mother compounded the problem.

If the Quran was the work of the Prophet Muhammad (PBUH), that dire point in history would have pushed him to make something up to defend his wife. But that was not the case. When his wife was slandered, no Quran was revealed to defend her, to the point that one could see the prophet looking up to the heavens, earnestly hoping for something.

Why was the situation as such? Because the Quran is the speech of God. The commandment of Allah. When Aishah was accused, Allah tested the Prophet Muhammad (PBUH), Aishah and the rest of the believers by withholding revelation. Until finally Allah freed Aishah and purified her honor with the revelation of the verses of *surah an-Nur* (21:1-26).

In fact, the revelation of the verses in *surah al-Kahf* about the companions of the cave, Zulqarnain and the matter of the soul in *surah al-Isra'*, all prove the same thing, that is, the Prophet Muhammad did not bring forth Quranic verses according to his whim or the direness of any situation, because it is not his speech.

It is the speech of Allah.

However, this point will seem irrelevant to those who reject Muslim literature, especially the hadiths of the Prophet Muhammad (PBUH).

The Universal Language of Mathematics

Looking for the truth of the Quran, verifying the claim that it contains the absolute truth, requires a more universal approach. A universal language that can be used by anyone capable of using their intellects.

Mathematics and the theory of probability fits the bill. We know that of the specialties of the Quran is that it contains amazing and accurate scientific facts. So many scientific findings discovered in our modern era, are mentioned in the Quran, a text that came into existence more than a thousand years ago at a time when man was not able to analyze nature and the universe accurately like we can today.

From where did those accurate scientific facts come?

"*Aghhh*.... It could just be a lucky guess!" says a group of those who do not believe or have not believed in the Quran.

Fine, let us, for argument's sake, accept the premise that the scientific facts in the Quran are a result of lucky guesses by its 'writer' named Muhammad.

Let's take a dice. What is the probability of getting number 3 with one throw? The answer is one over six (1/6). What is the probability of getting number 3 with two consecutive throws? The answer is one over six multiplied by one over six which equals one over thirty six (1/6 x 1/6 = 1/36).

Let us use this same theory to analyze the probability of multiple scientific facts occurring in the Quran.

For example, in the Quran, there is an explanation about the moon and the sun. If the prophet Muhammad (PBUH) wanted to make a guess whether the moon produced its own light, or reflects a light from another source, what is the probability of him making a right guess?

For sure, the probability is one over two (1/2). Whether it produces its own light, or if reflects light from another source.

That is a scientific fact.

What about other issues in the Quran? Like whether the earth revolves around the sun or vice versa. Or facts about what the human body is made of etc. If every single scientific fact in the Quran is said to be a result of lucky guesses by a man named Muhammad, then what is the probability of him making the right guess every single time?

Let us assume that there are only two possibilities for all scientific facts/theories and let's say there are 10 scientific facts (there are many more of course but for the sake of simplicity, let's just stick to 10) mentioned in the Quran. The probability of getting all of them right would be 1/2 x 1/2x 1/2 x 1/2 x ..... which would be 0.000 976 5625.... Or in other words, IMPOSSIBLE! Even in scientific studies, the cut off probability usually chosen to suggest something has not occurred by chance is 0.05, that is if an occurrence has a probability of 0.05 or less, then it is very very unlikely that the observation has occurred by chance.

It is a wonder beyond imagination that every scientific concept or fact mentioned in the Quran is ACCURATE and TRUE.

It means, the one speaking in the Quran must be someone who KNOWS VERY WELL about man and the universe. It cannot be anyone other than the Creator of man and the Creator of the universe Himself. That is God, that is Allah…. Allahu Akbar!

Such is how one uses probability theory to look for certainty regarding the Quran.

Science as a Tool

The point of this piece is not to proof that there are scientific facts in the Quran. That has become too cliché.

We need to go back to the thesis that whatever the Quran contains is meant as a GUIDANCE *(huda)*. Thus the presence of science in the Quran is to help men find guidance. If science is what one is familiar with, then use science as a means of arriving at certainty regarding the authenticity of the Quran.

Indeed, the most important question which needs to be answered by anyone who wishes to speak about the Quran is WHO IS BEHIND THE QURAN?

Is it really the speech of God?

Is it possible to hold a belief that it is the word of other than God?

If you find God after striving to answer this question, then you will realize that all your misconceptions about the Quran stemmed from your own ignorance, and not from any inherent defect of the Quran, because the Quran is the speech of Allah, the most Pure.

"We have certainly sent down to you a Book [i.e., the Qur'ān] in which is your mention. Then will you not reason?" *(al-Anbiyaa' 21:10)*

The Disease of
Religious Scepticism

"Why is he saying that? Does he not understand the Quran and Sunnah?" one of the attendees criticized the speaker delivering a talk.

"Has he not studied the *seerah*? Clueless about history perhaps?" added another person.

Everyone was angry with Habib Bourguiba.

Habib Bourguiba was the first President of Tunisia from 1957 to 1987. Bourguiba is often synonymized to Mustafa Kemal Ataturk because of his enthusiasm in westernization which he equated to modernization.

The issue is, in 1961, Habib Bourguiba legislated that civil servants of Tunisia cannot fast during the month of Ramadan. In order to prove his seriousness of this new ruling, he and members of his cabinet came on live television and ate lunch together during noon in Ramadan.

His excuse was simple; fasting reduces the productivity of the country!

Religious Cynicism

Habib Bourguiba's opinion on this matter can be categorized under what people would call religious scepticism.

Scepticism of or cynicism towards religion evolves in stages. Some are cynical about certain aspects of religious teachings like the ruling of washing a bowl licked by a dog using soil, or the ruling on covering the awrah, or even the ruling on males receiving twice the share of inheritance of women.

Sometimes, people are skeptical of religious institutions. For example, people may be anti-'mosque goers', or perhaps 'anti-religious bodies' like JAWI, JAKIM, JAIS (these are all religious bodies in Malaysia) and others. Not to mention those who are allergic to Islamic political parties, or even bodies with Islam as their central identity.

The third level is scepticism about religion as a whole. These people may not necessarily be anti-God or atheists, but they are cynical towards all religions for they consider them to be doctrines which are suspicious.

Whatever form religious scepticism takes, it is usually a response. When we say response, there must be something that developed gradually within, which caused the reaction. Most of the time, it does not occur naturally, but often as a response to something that happened earlier.

The Other Side of Habib Bourguiba's View

Going back to Habib Bourguiba's contention, some analysis of the matter is required.

Of course the Quran says otherwise, and the Sunnah says otherwise. In fact even history has proven otherwise, but Habib Bourguiba is not interested in all that. He based his opinion on what he witnessed in front of his eyes at the time.

Is it true that Muslims become more productive in Ramadan?

Let us leave Tunisia for a while and look at our situation in Malaysia.

In Ramadan, we are not able to have proper meetings. Everyone seems tired and in a daze, unable to come up with any good ideas. If there are any big projects to be discussed, everyone will push for the meetings to be postponed after *Eid*! In fact, outside Ramadan, we normally finish work at 5 in the evening; but in Ramadan we leave work at 4, all because we want to go the Ramadan Bazars!

So, are these not proofs that we indeed are not productive in Ramadan?

The problem with Habib Bourguiba is that he blamed fasting as the CAUSE, not the PEOPLE.

Strange

If you come across a Mercedes car overturned by the side of the road because it crashed into a lamppost, will you blame the Mercedes company?

"Mercedes is such a stupid company. How can they make cars which knock into lampposts!" says someone with the same mazhab as Habib Bourguiba.

Impossible.

Nobody will blame the Mercedes.

Everyone will blame the driver of the Mercedes.

"Does he not know how to drive? Even with a car as good as Mercedes he can go off the road and crash into the lamppost!" These would be words that are logical and make sense.

The mistake Habib Bourguiba made was blaming fasting and Ramadan as the cause of civil servants being unproductive. This is a very critical level of scepticism about religion.

Thus, if we do not agree with Habib Bourguiba's policy, then we should prove him wrong with our actions. This Ramadan, prove that you are productive, dynamic and actively working.

If we curse and swear at Habib Bourguiba with all our hearts because we disagree with his stance, but we ourselves are sluggish and unproductive during Ramadan, then all the verses of the Quran, or hadith, or historical facts we bring forth are merely rhetorical, and will encourage religious scepticism even more!

You can change that!

The Second Half of the *Taqwa* Cup

"You who have *iman!* Fasting is prescribed for you, as it was prescribed for those before you – so that hopefully you will have *taqwa*." *(al-Baqarah 2:183)*

We have entered the second half of Ramadan. The second half is usually the deciding half. If Ramadan were a football game, the second half is no longer a time to study the moves of the rival team, to deliberate about strategy merely in the mind or to run up and down the field aimlessly. Everyone should by this point know their roles and it is time to act and attack.

What is our score thus far this second half? If it is still 0-0, then we need to think about what is wrong. We have stayed away from disobedience, but perhaps have not increased our good works. What is more problematic is if we have stayed away from disobedience just because our 'friends' from among the jinn, devil, and men have become shackled, and not because we want to become closer to Allah. Forget not, that doing something for other than Allah is a form of showing off, leaving something for other than Allah too is a type of showing off.

If our score is now 1-0, then be thankful to Allah. But be cautious, for we may not yet be safe. Team *Nafs* is closing in on us, and may get a goal to match our score, while our defenses are weakening. Team *Nafs* is persistent, but we must move forward to penetrate its defensive ranks and score more goals so that we win by a large margin, not upon a fine line dividing victory and defeat.

Moreover, the *Eid* is approaching, and the fans of Team *Nafs* are overrunning the field with their large numbers. Their screams are becoming more terrifying. Do not lose heart because of them. We are the host team, we should at least win on our home ground.

But if you have entered the second half insipid, overtaken by time, then beware…. You are on the brink of defeat. The *Taqwa* Cup will soon fall into the hands of someone else, that is the hands of Team *Nafs* which does not actually know nor care about the value of the *Taqwa* Cup. It only wants to defeat your team, it wants to see that the *Taqwa* Cup does not end up in your hands.

Will we still be on the field next season? Nobody is brave enough to give an answer, for even the most skilled and accomplished coach will tell us that the only time we have in our hands, is now. The past is behind us, and the future is not within our reach. As for the time we have now, only the second half is left… is there still time to be nonchalant?

"Verily, Gabriel came to me and he said: Whoever reaches the month of Ramadan and he is not forgiven, then he will enter Hellfire and Allah will cast him far away, so say ameen. I said ameen." *(narrated by Ibnu Khuzaimah and Ibnu Hibban in his Sahih)*

The Question Is:
Where Is Your Ramadan?

"How strange. Rumour has it that they have been shackled. Shackled for the whole of Ramadan. Not just a rumour, but the Prophet (PBUH) himself told us about it. Al-Bukhaari (1899) and Muslim (1079) narrated from Abu Hurayrah (may Allah be pleased with him) that the Messenger of Allah (peace and blessings of Allah be upon him) said: "When Ramadaan comes, the gates of Paradise are opened, the gates of Hell are closed, and the devils are chained up."

The question is, how do we understand this statement?

Let us imagine a chained devil as if it were a dog on a leash. Can a dog on a leash not bite? Of course those who stay away from the dog will be safe, but what about those who go near the dog? Sit next to it, or taunt the dog which already seems to be angry because it has been leashed? It is not impossible for the silly person to be bitten. In fact, the bite might be worse because the dog is enraged.

When the devils are chained up in Ramadan, it only reduces their potential to incite man towards evil. In a hadith by Bukhari and Muslim, the Prophet (PBUH) said, "Satan flows through man like blood." And hence it has been commanded that we should restrict his pathway by fasting.

Ramadan restricts the potential of the devil. That said, for those who spend their Ramadan close to the favourite abode of devils, in places of *laghw* and disobedience where the jinns always visit, then what does one expect? When the devils are chained, man goes around 'looking' for them in their favourite places. Is this not equivalent to putting one's leg in front of a lion to be eaten?

We must realize that the sources of man's evil are external and internal. If the external source is the devil, then the internal one is man's own desire, which is perhaps the more dangerous one of the two.

"Have you seen him who takes his whims and desires to be his god…." *(Al- Jaathiyah 45:23)*

So after the doors of mercy have been opened, the gates of Hell shut and the devils chained, has not the path towards goodness been made wide enough to be walked upon and the path of evil difficult enough to be repelled from?

Who Else Should be Blamed?

If after all the incentives provided - to encourage man to change for the better - man still decides to commit evil, then who else should he blame if not himself?

Evil in the month of Ramadan is pure evil by the choice of man. There is almost no incitement from the devil in his choice to embrace evil. He has chosen to be bad and wretched on his own volition.

Just like fasting is a worship that is exclusively between Allah and His servant, in the same way, evil in the month of Ramadan will be punished by Him in an exclusive manner too.

The question then is, where will you spend your Ramadan? In places jinns and devils make their home? Or in places where the mercy of Allah descends because they are filled with those whose tongues are in constant remembrance of Him?

Beware of your steps. Remember the advice of Ubay to Umar about the road of *Taqwa*.

An Intended Uncertainty

Awaiting a night.

Is it just waiting or is it looking and hunting for it?

Lailatul Qadr is a night that will surely come. If waiting for it is just about staying up, then those who keep their eyes open without doing anything are the lucky ones when the night passes them by. Certainly, it is not a night of waiting, but a night of hunting and searching.

Who knows, it could the 21st night, or maybe the 23rd, or perhaps any of the other odd nights that *Lailatul Qadr* will be gifted to us.

The Prophet (PBUH) went through nine Ramadans after it was made obligatory, and each year he would mention a different night for *Lailatul Qadr*, a situation from which our scholars have deduced that *Lailatul Qadr* is a gift granted to us in one of the last 10 nights of Ramadan.

"Why was it not decreed as one specific night every year?" someone asked.

"Which night do you suggest?" I responded with another question.

"The 27th night would be good."

"Thus shall the oil and lamp sellers gain huge profits for that night!" I joked.

"*Erk*, didn't expect that you'd go there ustaz," he said.

E-Reading Confusion

I read an article written in an e-reading website, rejecting the hadiths of the Prophet (PBUH) including the ones relating to *Lailatul Qadr*. The writer argues that the search for *Lailatul Qadr* is useless because all the hadiths on the subject are contradictory to one another. The fact of the matter is that the hadiths are a collection of dialogues and explanations of the Prophet (PBUH) about Lailatulqadr which occurred at least nine times in his life as a prophet. Each of those hadiths was said in a different year, not that they contradict one another as this anti-hadith group claims.

The question arises, what if this uncertainty is intended? It is not ignorance, but there is a great secret behind it all.

Wage-earning vs Self-employment

It is easier for us to analogize this matter: A person who is a wage earner versus one who is self-employed. As to the one who is a wage earner, his wages are fixed at the end of every month. Whether he is productive or not, he earns his wages. In fact, if this person sleeps during working hours in his office and leaves work early because of Ramadan, he would still earn the same wages. Something certain and fixed, it appears, can affect one's earnestness and productivity, because he has taken for granted all that he been blessed with.

This is quite different to one who is self-employed. His income is very dependent on his effort, diligence and productivity. If he works hard, he earns more. If he is works little, his income is compromised.

Uncertainty is the secret to diligence and hard work needed for a good outcome. Uncertainty + hard work = advancement, that is the equation. That is the wisdom of uncertainty.

Multifold

Thirty days may be too long a period to search for *Lailatul Qadr*. Therefore, Islam tells us to increase our efforts to chase that special and uncertain night in the last 10 nights of Ramadan. Because it will happen on a night that is not known, those who wish to succeed will multiply their efforts to look for it. *Lailatul Qadr*, the Night of Power.

That diligence is what completes the process of *TAQWA*.

It is a diligence that is needed for a life that has a limit which is unknown. Death is certain, its time is uncertain. Between the certainty and uncertainty of death, a *mu'min* strives to develop his life.

With the thought that our opportunity for good actions will come to end at an uncertain point in time, the Prophet (PBUH) reminded us to always perform our prayers as if it is our "FAREWELL PRAYER". We must endeavor to establish each prayer as if it is our last, because death is uncertain, and will always arrive between two prayers....

It is an uncertainty that makes diligence and change compelling.

"Verily, Gabriel came to me and he said: Whoever reaches the month of Ramadan and he is not forgiven, then he will enter Hellfire and Allah will cast him far away, so say ameen. I said ameen." *(narrated by Ibnu Khuzaimah and Ibnu Hibban in his Sahih)*

Quickly We Must
Sow Our Seeds

It feels heavy. It is difficult for me to conceal this. Conceal what? Certainly not the rights of another. I am not concealing knowledge, news or anything that is obligatory for me to reveal and propagate.

What I am concealing is something complex. I was taught by my teacher, that an ordinary smile is a smile when one is happy. However, an extraordinary smile is a smile to make others happy. The heart drowns in sorrow, the spirit is anxious, but for the sake of making others happy, I learn to loyally wear a smile on my face.

Yes, this is what I find difficult to conceal. The anxiety and sadness behind my smile on the morning of the *Eid*. The *Eid* reminds me of many sad incidents and I find it strange that people can jump around joyfully when Shawwal comes, just as the sun sets on the last day of Ramadan. The month of hunger is gone, the month of 'this is not allowed and that is not allowed'. The ordinary months are back. Ordinary months full of extraordinarily ordinary things!

This Ramadan, I feel like I have swallowed a bitter pill of the realities around me. The world has been inflicted with all kinds of disasters. If America is hit by a hurricane, it is not difficult to reflect upon the reason of why it happened. But what about Acheh and Kashmir? I am trying to make sense of the cause and effect of these disasters, and each time I think about it, I am overwhelmed with sadness. As if natural disasters are not enough, man too is drifting further away from God. It is as if Ramadan has no meaning nor value. The world cannot get any worse or tragic than what it is today.

We Do Not Need to be Paranoid

I stare into space reminiscing the picture below:

This is a picture that I have taken from the book "Umru Ummatil Islam wa Qurbu Dzuhi al-Mahdi 'Alayhi as-Salaam (1996)' authoured by Amin Muhammad Jamaluddin (al-Maktabah at-Taufiqiyyah, Cairo, Egypt). It has been translated into Malay with the title 'Umur Umat Islam, Kedatangan Imam Mahdi dan Munculnya Dajjal (The age of the Muslim *Ummah*, the coming of *Imam Mahdi* and the appearance of *Dajjal*)' (Published by Cendekia, Jakarta, Indonesia). It is a synopsis of the events leading up to Judgment Day from authentic hadiths as well as other hadiths which although are not of the same level as authentic hadiths, are still valid for reference.

Whether we like it or not, these events are definitely going to happen. Reminding people about the Day of Judgment is not a type of *bid'ah* (innovation) to create fear and panic, but it is a method that is employed again and again by the Quran. Even the Prophet (PBUH) always reminded his companions and the rest of the ummah to be prepared, because his coming (PBUH) marks the beginning of the end.

But I should stress that we should not be paranoid about reminders of Judgment Day or reminders of death. We are not taught to fear death and the Day of Judgment, but instead to embrace them with a positive attitude.

This is what one can learn from *Lailatul Qadr*. Allah the Most High decrees that it should fall on a night that is not known except for some tips on when we should look for it. A thing uncertain, if looked at positively, can help us to achieve excellence. We do not know when we shall die, when Judgment Day will be, when the victory of Islam will happen, when *Lailatul Qadr* occurs every Ramadan and so on.

All of this, if embraced with a positive attitude as mentioned earlier, will encourage us to work hard and increase our effort. In fact, perhaps this is why Islam encourages us to be involved in business. Business is not like earning wages. Earning wages makes us complacent in our comfort zones. Whether we are productive or not, the wages come in.

But for those involved in business, if they work hard, then insya Allah they will take home much. The important thing is, maximizing our effort due to uncertainty will make us successful.

Giving without Wanting any Return

This is what I hope I have gained from the 'reminders' about Judgment Day in the form of the unfortunate events that occurred before the *Eid* this year. I believe, to plan for the Hereafter, I need to learn from the philosophy of our ancestors who used to plant durian trees. They knew they would not be able to taste the fruits thereof, but they planted the trees regardless so their children and grandchildren after them would be able to taste and enjoy them. They gave without any feeling of wanting anything in return.... Except for the reward for their good deed from Allah alone.

Maybe I will not live to encounter the anarchy during the wars of *Ya'juj and Ma'juj* (Gog and Magog), *Dajjal* (the anti-Christ) and others. However, it may occur in the lifetime of my son or perhaps my grandchildren, and so it is my duty to raise my kids with a good knowledge of God because I worry, when the *Mahdi* arrives, whether they will become part of the armies of Tawhid, or the followers of the lying *Dajjal*..... Allah.... We must be quick to sow our seeds, before Judgment Day arrives, before we die.

Weep over the departure of Ramadan because its passing without any forgiveness from Allah means we are on the edge of the Fire of Hell. "Ameen, ameen, ameen...." said the Prophet (PBUH).

The Dilemma of *Istiqamah* After Ramadan

"Hmm, these courses are such a waste of time. I bet my bottom dollar any realization will last max 2 weeks, then it's back to normal!" said one worker who seemed pessimistic about the course he was attending.

Perhaps he failed to realize, that it is not only in the case of manmade courses that people face this problem of persistence. How difficult it is for people who have done the Hajj to retain their 'like a new born baby' status until death takes them?

And what about this intensive course called Ramadan that Allah Himself designed? Does not the same issue arise?

The problem is not whether the course is manmade or divine, but it is the nature of man that has highs and lows. Thus, the question of how one transforms after a course, is no trivial question!

What After Ramadan?

What after Ramadan? A heavy question that will be repeated.

"Back to square one?" a tiresome probability which will bring forth feelings of guilt.

"Is it possible to remain good and continue being better?" a difficult question that needs great consideration. Everything becomes a source of reflection during these last nights of Ramadan. Shawwal is welcomed with a 1001 questions, all of them about *ISTIQAMAH*. That is the question – *Istiqamah*, the consistency to remain good and become better.

A Peculiarity

Very strange indeed, that people throng the mosques for the OPTIONAL taraweeh prayer but are so lax when it comes to the five OBLIGATORY prayers.

How peculiar again that Ramadan is filled with the Quran, but the Quran is abandoned for the remaining 11 months.

Truly odd it is when people observe their awrah in Ramadan but behave as if they were godless during the other months. It is not uncommon to find people who fulfill the obligation to fast in Ramadan, but fail to fulfill the higher obligation of PRAYER.

All of these are some of our peculiarities. A strangeness that arises from how differently we behave in Ramadan when compared to outside of it. Therein lies the complexity of the question of *istiqamah*.

The Burden of *Istiqamah*

Abu Juhayfa (may Allah be pleased with him) said: 'The people said: "O Messenger of Allah! We see the signs of old age (grey hairs) beginning to show on you?"The Messenger of God (PBUH) replied "*Surah Hud* and her sisters have made me old". *[Shamaail Tirmidhi]*

That is the burden of *surah Hud*, a *surah* that speaks about *istiqamah* i.e. when one's heart is touched with Imaan, then one should live with Imaan and die with Imaan.

How can what we learn in Ramadan last until our last breath?

The Pillars of *Istiqamah*

There is no room for conjecture when it comes to *istiqamah*, but one must follow its pillars which Allah has revealed in *surah Hud*.

We should try to adapt those pillars to Ramadan for indeed Ramadan is a training to produce *istiqamah*.

Allah the Most High Most Glorious says in *surah Hud* verses 112 to 115:

﴿ فَٱسْتَقِمْ كَمَآ أُمِرْتَ وَمَن تَابَ مَعَكَ وَلَا تَطْغَوْاْ إِنَّهُۥ بِمَا تَعْمَلُونَ بَصِيرٌ ۝ وَلَا تَرْكَنُوٓاْ إِلَى ٱلَّذِينَ ظَلَمُواْ فَتَمَسَّكُمُ ٱلنَّارُ وَمَا لَكُم مِّن دُونِ ٱللَّهِ مِنْ أَوْلِيَآءَ ثُمَّ لَا تُنصَرُونَ ۝ وَأَقِمِ ٱلصَّلَوٰةَ طَرَفِيِ ٱلنَّهَارِ وَزُلَفًا مِّنَ ٱلَّيْلِ إِنَّ ٱلْحَسَنَٰتِ يُذْهِبْنَ ٱلسَّيِّـَٔاتِ ذَٰلِكَ ذِكْرَىٰ لِلذَّٰكِرِينَ ۝ وَٱصْبِرْ فَإِنَّ ٱللَّهَ لَا يُضِيعُ أَجْرَ ٱلْمُحْسِنِينَ ﴾

"So remain on a right course as you have been commanded, [you] and those who have turned back with you [to Allāh], and do not transgress. Indeed, He is Seeing of what you do.

And do not incline toward those who do wrong, lest you be touched by the Fire, and you would not have other than Allāh any protectors; then you would not be helped.

And establish prayer at the two ends of the day and at the approach of the night. Indeed, good deeds do away with misdeeds. That is a reminder for those who remember.

And be patient, for indeed, Allāh does not allow to be lost the reward of those who do good."

(Quran 11: 112–115)

The First Pillar: Do Not Go to Excesses in Religion

وَلَا تَطْغَوْاْ

"Do not transgress (lit. exceed the bounds)"

It is quite common for us to meet people who go to excesses in religion. There is no need for extreme examples. Enough it is as a transgression that people do more than what Allah has commanded, in the belief, that making things difficult for themselves by going to excesses is a way to attain TAQWA.

With regards to Ramadan, the earliest excesses in religion were done by some companions who wanted to fast continuously for 3 months from Rajab to Ramadan, an act which was criticized by the Prophet (PBUH) himself.

The Prophet (PBUH) went even further by reminding us to break our fast early and delay our *sahoor*.

"Calm down man, *sahoor* is not compulsory. Let's eat now so we don't have to wake up so early. It's twelve o'clock anyway," said one youngster to his friend.

"Aww man, I knew the roads would be jammed up! It's fine, I won't die if I break my fast half an hour late," murmured a man in his car, stuck in traffic.

The habit of abandoning the Sunnah of *sahoor* and delaying breaking fast especially because of problems one can already expect, like bad rush hour traffic, is against the reminder of the Prophet (PBUH). `Amr Ibn al-`Aas reported that the Messenger of Allah (PBUH) said: "The distinction between our fasting and the fasting of the people of the book [Jews and Christians] is the taking of *Sahoor*". *[Muslim]*

And in another hadith: "The people will not cease to be upon good as long as they hasten in breaking the fast." *[Bukhari and Muslim]*

So significant is the issue of observing *sahoor* and hastening to break the fast, that the Prophet linked both these acts to our identities as Muslims which make us distinct from the Jews and Christians. In other words, he equated fasting earlier than usual and longer than usual to following the mentality and tendency of the People of the Book, the Jews and Christians.

What kind of tendency is that? That is the tendency to commit excesses in religion.

Much of the destruction of Jewish and Christian teachings revolves around their excesses in religion. Just look at the issue of celibacy, where marriage is forbidden just so one can attain closeness to God. Just look at the deification of the Prophet Jesus by the Christians who lifted him to the status of God. There are many other examples of how a deviated interpretation and understanding which transgress the limits set by God brings forth destruction.

Thus, in Ramadan, we should rectify our tendency to believe that difficult and heavy deeds are the best means to achieve TAQWA.

Indeed, going to excesses with respect to fasting by abandoning *sahoor*, delaying *iftar*, fasting continuously beginning Rajab or even the whole year.... All these transgressions of the limits set by God pose a great challenge to our effort to be consistent.

Therefore, moderate acts, or even small but consistent acts are the best. The best deeds are those that obey the minimum and maximum limits set by Allah because "Truly, going to excesses and falling short are brothers," said Shaykh Fadhl Hasan Abbas when discussing this issue *(Al-Khumasiyyat al-Mukhtarah fi Tahdhib an-Nafs al-Ammarah)*.

The explanations in the Quran often pair being excessive with being corrupt – transgression is the cause of corruption. The trait of transgressing *(taghut* and *tughyan)* is used to describe the people of 'Ad and Thamud, Pharaoh and Qarun and it is their transgression that justified their destruction. And this does not stop at morality and character, but is true even in the case of the laws of nature that Allah has set down *(sunnatullah)*. With excessive eating and drinking, the body is destroyed, while with excessive consumption of resources, the earth and by extension man are destroyed. Excessiveness is not compatible with nature, and that is why it is cursed by the Owner of nature.

Do not be excessive in religion whether it be in thought, in deeds, in principles or even in feelings.

We all know the story of a few companions who wanted to pray at night without sleeping, fast without breaking their fasts, and even worship without marrying but were chided by the Prophet (PBUH) because that is not how mankind should believe in God.

Everything must be in balance.

Fast, but break the fast. Stand up at night and pray, but allocate time for sleep too. Worship as much as possible, but marry also. If we refuse this balance, then "You are not of my people," said the Prophet (PBUH).

The Second Pillar: Do Not Incline Towards Those Who Do Wrong

Going to excesses is a form of oppression, because it places thoughts and actions on a scale beyond what has been determined by Allah. In that same vein, we should also stay away from oppression so we may be in line with the second pillar, that is, do not incline towards those who do wrong i.e. those who commit oppression.

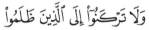

"And do not incline toward those who do wrong…"

Hasan al-Basri once said, "The religion has been built upon two 'do nots'. Do not transgress and do not incline toward those who do wrong."

What Kind of Inclination?

"Inclined in two ways. Either inclined towards the principle and emotion, or inclined by being dependent," explained Shaykh Fadhl Hasan Abbas in his book *Al-Khumasiyyat al-Mukhtarah fi Tahdhib an-Nafs al-Ammarah* which I have in my hands.

The first inclination that destroys *istiqamah* is the inclination of our hearts and emotions towards those who do wrong, those who are oppressors (zalim). Instead of resisting, the heart inclines to such persons for various reasons like feeling indebted for a prior favour, or having a weak resolve.

The second inclination however goes back to the meaning of *RUKN* in the verse above. *Rukn* is a place something leans against depending on it, like how the structure of a house 'leans' on the pillars. Thus, of those who are inclined toward oppressors are those who depend on them whether it be for food, drink, status, job or any other reason.

Who Are Those Who Are *Zalim*?

Because it is mentioned in general terms, Shaykh Fadhl Hasan Abbas prefers to retain its general context. The zalim can be a non-Muslim oppressor, or he could also be a Muslim oppressor. Thus the consistency of a Mu'min is tied to refraining from being inclined to such persons.

The *zalim* is he who associates partners with God, who commits disobedience and who oppresses other people.

Perhaps in the context of our current life, it could refer to our old friends who invite us to join them for a night out at the pub, or to play golf until we miss our prayer and other duties. We must be wary of inclining towards them after we have changed for the better, post-Ramadan.

It should not be the case that after changing for the better we abandon our old friends completely. No, that is not the way. Who knows, perhaps our change might be an impetus for them to change too by the permission of Allah. But in our endeavor to preserve the friendship, we should not incline towards their wrongdoing i.e. their disobedient acts towards Allah. There should not be a compromise on our values just because we do not want to hurt their feelings. If we compromise our values, then our ability for *istiqamah* will fail and we will no longer be able to maintain any positive change we have achieved.

They need to be embraced for the purpose of *da'wah*, but that embrace should not be to the extent of condoning their behaviour. If the question is about methodology, there are many ways. But to see evil and wrongdoing as evil and wrongdoing, should be a clear principle we must hold on to.

The wrongdoer is he who oppresses.

The wrongdoer is he who associates partners with God.

The wrongdoer is he who holds the wrong principles, putting things not at their appropriate place.

The Tale of the Tailor

Sufyan al-Thawri was once asked by someone, "I work as a tailor for a tyrant. Am I considered as one who is inclined towards oppressors (referring to this verse in *surah Hud*)?"

Sufyan al-Thawri replied," Nay! You are an oppressor yourself. As for the one who is inclined towards the oppressor, it is he who sells the needle for you to sew!"

That is how severe Sufyan al-Thawri's warning was to that man.

Istiqamah is strongly associated with balance, like one who is walking on a straight but dilapidated bridge who must focus his concentration wholly on balancing himself lest he falls down, even if the bridge is straight.

وَلَا تَرْكَنُوٓاْ إِلَى ٱلَّذِينَ ظَلَمُواْ فَتَمَسَّكُمُ ٱلنَّارُ وَمَا لَكُم مِّن دُونِ ٱللَّهِ مِنْ أَوْلِيَآءَ ثُمَّ لَا تُنصَرُونَ ﴿١١٣﴾

"And do not incline toward those who do wrong, lest you be touched by the Fire, and you would not have other than Allāh any protectors; then you would not be helped."

Those who incline towards the *zaalimoon* will not be thrown into the Fire, but the Fire will smite them because of the inability of their hearts to reject the oppression, something Allah forbade even upon Himself. Thus they will have no helper in the Hereafter, after being disgraced in this world because there is not helper for one whom Allah has washed His hands from.

It is hoped that our attendance to the mosque in Ramadan has given us the opportunity to be in the company of good people with whom we should spend most of our time so we can attain *husnul khatimah*.

The Third Pillar: Establish Prayer

وَأَقِمِ ٱلصَّلَوٰةَ طَرَفِي ٱلنَّهَارِ وَزُلَفًا مِّنَ ٱلَّيۡلِ إِنَّ ٱلۡحَسَنَٰتِ يُذۡهِبۡنَ
ٱلسَّيِّـَٔاتِۚ ذَٰلِكَ ذِكۡرَىٰ لِلذَّٰكِرِينَ ۝

"And establish prayer at the two ends of the day and at the approach of the night. Indeed, good deeds do away with misdeeds. That is a reminder for those who remember."

Istiqamah leans upon PRAYER. Prayer connects us to Allah the Most High continuously. During the day and at night, prayer functions to make a person realize that his life is not godless but that he is always connected to God.

The night prayer of Ramadan (*tarawih*) serves as a training for us to make prayer a habit. It should not be just a form of servitude, but a form of rest too.

Resting with prayer? What a strange notion.

Strange only if we forget that it is during prayer that we speak to Allah the Most Loving and Compassionate. The question is, do we reciprocate that compassion and love? The answer lies in whether the prayer is a form of rest for ourselves, or otherwise.

People in love can talk on the phone for hours on end, without getting bored of talking or listening. The power of love can make difficulty lose its burdensome nature and transform it into a sort of favour and rest.

If we feel burdened due to prayer, it means we do no love the One who is Most Loving!

Thus we must ask ourselves, is it possible to have *istiqamah* with regard to His commands when we do not love Him?

A gentle reminder for us all. The prayer is obligatory as long as we are conscious. There should not be a moment when we absolve ourselves of prayer just because we're unwell. It would be a terrible end for one who prayed his whole life and then left the prayer a few days before he died just because he was unwell. Are we able to make sure that we guard our prayer until our last breath?

Allah! Allah!

The Fourth Pillar: Be Patient

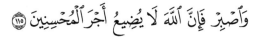

"And be patient, for indeed, Allāh does not allow to be lost the reward of those who do good."

Being patient throughout Ramadan translates to controlling ourselves and our actions.

Let us be patient when it comes to our effort to worship, and to seek knowledge so we may become knowledgeable.

Let us be patient in *da'wah*, so that any rejection we face will not cause us to look for a shortcut that will jeopardize our *istiqamah*.

Patience protects us from emotional tendencies that lead to extremism. Patience guards us from going to excesses with regard to the knowledge we have gained, because knowledge and wealth are two hot potatoes in our grasp. Be patient, so knowledge leads to humility and wealth leads to gratitude.

Let it not happen that you transgress because of your knowledge.

Let it not happen that you transgress because of your wealth.

In the same way, let it not happen that you transgress because of your power.

Be patient. There is no patience except by Allah, no patience except by being in close proximity to Allah, no patience except by being patient for Allah. Above all, do not ever try to be patient FROM Allah i.e. be patient in trying our best to get away from Him.

How heavy is this word *istiqamah*. It is not surprising then the Prophet's (PBUH) hairs turned grey thinking about it.

Let us together REVIVE THE SPIRIT OF RAMADAN.

A Christmas Emotion Tragedy

"Ustaz, what is the ruling on buying a Santa Claus doll?" a student asked after I finished my talk on the 40 Hadith, that night.

The Clinical Science Institue, NUI Galway is always merry with the presence of medical students who are keen to study their religion.

"*Err*, why do you want to buy that doll?" I replied with a question.

"Its cute ustaz. It almost feels like a wasted opportunity if I don't buy one. Not to mention how cheap it is!" he said.

"Emm, I think let us put aside the question about its ruling. Now imagine this. Let's say Rasulullah (PBUH) came to visit you in your house. If he were to sit in your living room, would you want the Santa Claus doll to be there? Or would you hide it?" I tried an alternative 'therapy'.

The student who asked, as well as his friends laughed.

"So, do you still want to buy it?" Masri teased that student.

On the authority of an-Nawas bin Sam'an (may Allah be pleased with him), the Prophet (peace be upon him) said: "Righteousness is in good character, and wrongdoing is that which wavers in your soul, and which you dislike people finding out about." *[collected by Muslim]*

Indeed, there is no need to search for rulings. This advice by the Prophet (PBUH) should be enough. If something we wish to do causes a feeling of anxiety and a desire to keep that act secret so that people do not know about it, then *insha-Allah*, that act is SINFUL.

December in the West

Being in Ireland in December can be bewildering. The Christmas celebration is no simple affair. In Belfast, Galway and Dublin, the main streets are already beautifully decorated as early as the 1st of December. There are sales in every supermarket. Santa Claus and his reindeer are all over the place. Who doesn't become excited with all this?

Everything is about Christmas. Santa Claus, gifts, shopping and credit cards!

Merry *Kufr!*

That said, I do not think there is any sense of religiosity behind Christmas celebrations. There are hardly any elements that invite Christians whether Catholics or Protestants, to draw themselves closer to their 'god', to Jesus Christ. Christmas is merely about celebrations, joy and fun, coupled with disappointment and sadness amongst the homeless.

Any purpose of Christmas celebrated today is far away from God, Jesus or the Bible. The idea of festivities and the obligation to have gatherings as a family dominate the Christmas atmosphere. It is for this reason that Shaykh Abdul Rahim Green, when he gave his talk in Dublin mosque, expressed his disappointment at the attitude of Muslims who busy themselves wishing Merry Christmas to Christians.

"Do you know how we feel, the Muslim reverts who were once Christians? When you say Happy Christmas to them, what we hear is just Merry *Kufr*, Happy *Shirk!*" he said.

Reversed

"How strange is it, in Malaysia youngsters fill bus and train stations before the *Eid* to go back to their hometowns, while here the elderly fill the stations to go visit their kids in their homes," I expressed my thoughts to Nasreel, our housemate in London, amazed by the sight of the elderly lining up to get onto the trains in Paddington Station, going towards the west of England.

"This is normal ustaz. Londoners, as they say!" he responded smiling.

The view in Heathrow is not much different. Mothers and fathers make it compulsory upon themselves to visit their children at their homes.

A Sadness Not Because of Religion

Christmas is also a day of suffering for those who have no family. Sometimes I feel sad seeing those who wander the streets of Belfast, and make homes of them. Who knows how they sleep, or where they get food. Most of them find escape from the troubles of life through addiction. Addiction to alcohol, drugs or sex.... Who knows!

Indeed many of them commit suicide during Christmas. The Christmas Carols that are sung are like a fire that burns their souls. They have no family to go back to, isolated and lonely, finishing the remnants of their meaningless lives. What they feel may be similar to what some of us feel when we hear the *Takbir* during *Eid*. Sad..... with a sadness that does not stem from religiosity.

Christmas and *Eid al-Fitr*

Sometimes I think the 'fate' of Christmas and *Eid al-Fitr* are not that different. Both are awaited for by believers of their respective religions, but not to Glorify God. Christmas and *Eid al-Fitr* are but yearly festivals. Christmas and *Eid al-Fitr* are days that bring forth a feeling of melancholy not because of reflection about one's sinful self, or because of the departure of Ramadan and its days of forgiveness. Christmas and *Eid al-Fitr* are days when city folk try to redeem themselves for the sin of forgetting about their families and ties of kinship all this while.

The tears are not tears of faith. The smiles and laughter have nothing to do with God. Whether it be Christians and their Christmas or Muslims and their *Eid*, religion has become mere tradition.

Christmas in Malaysia

I feel disgusted watching the city folk in Kuala Lumpur busying themselves with Christmas. *Cekodok pisang* with a Santa hat. People jumping around 'ho ho ho'-ing away in shopping complexes. What has been imported to our society in conjunction with Christmas is not an awareness to appreciate religion. It only demonstrates the poverty of self-esteem amongst our people who are bent on trying to Westernize themselves.

When watching local television programs, I become even more disgusted at the conduct of 'urban people' who are so desperate to become Westernized. Desperados!

This is the product of Western education, as was desired by Thomas Babington Macaulay, a British Education Officer who designed the education systems of imperialized countries like India. What he wanted was to nurture a people who were 'Indian in blood and colour, English in taste".

In Malaysia, we have many Malays who have Malay blood and are Malay coloured, Chinese with Chinese blood and are Chinese coloured, as well as Indians with Indian blood and are

Indian coloured, but have the thinking and taste of the West. This group, whether they have changed their hair colour to blonde or otherwise, have never been accepted by the West as Westerners. It is they themselves who are mad about all things Western, making a fool of themselves, embarrassed to be described as Eastern or Muslims.

In fact, I think the zealousness of Malaysians in leaving Islam for Christianity, is not because they are convinced of the doctrines and teachings of the Bible. The phenomenon of apostasy happening now is an effort to free one's self from the fetters of religion, so one is not punished for the sin of imbibing alcohol or fornication and adultery. Why? Because Christianity is propagated as an accommodative religion which offers forgiveness, which gives 'hope', while the sinful person in Islam, like an adulterer, is a target for stoning or lashing.

To me, apostasy and Christmas celebrations are a manifestation of pseudo-religiosity, not a true one. The phenomenon of Muslim *murtadds* is essentially a wave of people moving from a true religion to a pseudo-religion. It does not raise the banner of Christianity, but is just an excuse to be free from religion and God.

Sigh.... Malaysia and her tendency to produce slaves of entertainment and festivals. Her people want to falsify all religions by removing questions of faith and the search for truth, to mere culture and tradition, traditions which have nothing to do with the East, nor with Islam.

It was narrated on the authority of Abu Sa'eed that the Prophet, said: "You will certainly follow the ways of those who came before you hand span by hand span, cubit by cubit, to the extent that if they enter the hole of a lizard, you will enter it too.' We said, 'O Messenger of Allah, (do you mean) the Jews and the Christians?' He said: 'Who else?'" *[Al-Bukhari and Muslim]*

The height of this insanity is when a Malay Muslim fasts and breaks his fast with liquor as was reported in a local newspaper in the Ramadan of 1429. It is a painful burden, thinking about the religiosity of man, or rather the lack thereof, at the end of times.

Eid al-Fitr - Who Are the *'Aideen* and *Faaizeen*?

"*Selamat Hari Lebaran, minal 'aideen wal faaizeen....*" The same song was played repeatedly on the radio in conjunction with the *Eid*. My heart felt disturbed at those words of Siti Muslihah which have long been forgotten. The same words are crafted onto *Eid* cards whether they be electronic or paper.

But have we actually thought deeply about the meaning of those greetings? How great the implication behind those words? Or has it too become a meaningless greeting like how '*Assalamualaikum*' has, void of any prayer, or '*insha-Allah*' that is often used as a cover to break promises? This phenomenon of empty words has long been in existence. Hassan al-Banna often used to begin his speeches with the following words, "I welcome you with the welcoming greeting of Islam, a greeting whose origins is with Allah, full of goodness and blessings, people use it as a habit, while we say it as an act of worship, *Assalamualaikum wa Rahmatullahi wa Barakatuh*."

As servants of God, we must always remember that the only purpose Allah created us is to worship Him. Everything we do must be a form of worship. If we live for 60 years and sleep 8 hours day, then we must ensure that our 20 years of sleeping is considered worship. If all of our actions are allowed to go to waste, then we will be bankrupt when we face Allah on the plains of *Mahsyar*. Therefore all good habits must be elevated in quality so they can qualify as worship. If habits can fulfill at least 6 core criteria, then we can present them as worship before Allah on the Day of Judgment. The six criteria are:

1. A correct, good and precise intention.

2. The habit or any activity for that matter must be something that is permissible.

3. Its execution is not mixed with any elements which are contradictory to the laws of Islam

4. It is done in the best way (*itqan* and optimum)

5. Priorities must be observed. General acts of worship cannot replace optional and obligatory acts of worship.

6. The effects or outcomes of the act are good.

Thus, the greetings we utter during this period of festivities must be meaningful. In fact, the implication of other greetings like "Happy Deepavali" and the like must be scrutinized.

I remember a talk given by Brother Abdul Raheem Green when he visited Ireland some time ago. One of the things he said was, "When we say 'Wishing you a Merry Christmas, 'Have a nice Christmas' and others, actually we are saying 'Wishing you a Happy *Shirk*', 'Have a nice *Kufr!*' You may not feel that way, but we who used to be Christians and have embraced Islam, feel that way when we hear such greetings, because we know the value of faith and the danger of *kufr!*"

I do not wish to discuss the ruling of greeting non-Muslims during their festivities. Let the question of rulings be left to those who are more knowledgeable in the matter. What I wish to point out is our culture of just saying things without thinking deeply about what we are saying. If this disease is not treated perhaps it will start affecting even our prayer whereby we recite the Quran and utter *dhikr* without actually caring to know what they mean.

Returning to the Fitrah

Going back to the question of minal 'aideen wal faaizeen earlier. It is a great utterance.

I mentioned previously that these words are uttered to congratulate ourselves on our achievement of fulfilling the duties of Ramadan and success in completing its educational training, while we bid farewell to this great month feeling like we are on a high place of honor. We feel this way because we have managed to suppress our *nafs*, and bring our hearts back to life besides lightening our bodies for more worship. In fact, we have changed our attitude to what is better, in line with the original traits Allah created us with. Yes, we have returned to the *FITRAH*, 'returned to the path of Allah'. This is the meaning of *'AIDEEN*, that is, those who have returned.

Those who have successfully reignited their *FITRAH* which has been caged all this while in the cage of *nafs* and ignorance are the true victors.

"He has succeeded who purifies it (*nafs*)" *(Ash-Syams 91:9)*

This is the meaning of *al-Faaizeen* that we keep uttering.

So let us look in the mirror and take a good look at ourselves. Have we returned to our fitrah after this Ramadan? Do we have any of the traits of the believers mentioned in many places in the Quran? And have we truly succeeded?

If not, then all these utterances, far from being congratulatory, are actually taunts and insults. We insult ourselves when we say these words but have not done anything to fulfill their meanings. May we truly return to the *FITRAH* before returning to Allah because it is they who are the *FAIZEEN* who will attain *AL-FALAH*.

Eid al-Fitr:
Celebrating Our Islam

How quickly time flies. Without realizing, Ramadan has left us. Will there be an opportunity for us to witness the next Ramadan? Only Allah knows. We are reminded of the incident where the Prophet (PBUH) walked up the stairs of his pulpit in his mosque saying ameen to each prayer made by Jibril (upon whom is peace).

Abu Huraira reported: The Prophet, peace and blessings be upon him, ascended the pulpit and he said, "Ameen, ameen, ameen." It was said, "O Messenger of Allah, you ascended the pulpit and said ameen, ameen, ameen." The Prophet said, "Verily, Gabriel came to me and he said: Whoever reaches the month of Ramadan and he is not forgiven, then he will enter Hellfire and Allah will cast him far away, so say ameen. I said ameen." *(Sahih Ibn Hibban 915 – authenticated by al-Albani)*

Is this warning not frightening enough? How far have we gone in utilizing Ramadan with purposeful worship so we can earn the forgiveness of Allah? Have we managed to achieve any taqwa?

Only our own small hearts can answer as to how much effort we have put in during the month. Those who worked hard should praise Allah while those who were lackadaisical should mourn with a deep mourning their lack of interest in Ramadan. If Ramadan cannot help us improve ourselves, then which other day, week or month can be our saviour?

When Ramadan Passes

After the passing of Ramadan, the pious predecessors always used to beseech Allah up to six months after Ramadan to accept the good deeds they did in that month. It is not difficult to ascertain whether the good deeds during Ramadan have been accepted. If after Ramadan, our obedience to Allah continues, then that is a great bestowal from Allah. This is what Allah commands us to do:

"And worship your Lord until there comes to you the certainty [i.e., death]." *(Al-Hijr 15:99)*

On the contrary, if worship is seasonal like football, durians or fever, then cursed is the end of such worship. There are many signs which show that a person's deeds have been rejected by Allah, like being able to attend *tarawih* prayers which are optional at the mosque everyday of Ramadan but failing to go to the mosque for the five obligatory prayers. Or one whose tongue is continuously wet from reciting the Quran and *dhikr* of Allah in Ramadan, but then he returns to false and vain music which lead to nothing but the wrath of Allah. May Allah protect us from this sort of accursedness.

After Ramadan, we should not forget the Sunnah of fasting six days in Shawwal. Its status is like the rawatib prayers which accompany the obligatory prayers. It serves to compensate for any deficiencies in our Ramadan fast.

"You who have iman! fasting is prescribed for you, as it was prescribed for those before you – so that hopefully you will have taqwa." *(al-Baqarah 2:183)*

The *Madrasa* of Ramadan

'Enrollment' in the *Madrasa* of Ramadan should be utilized as well as possible so we may attain taqwa. Those who travel or live in a foreign land will usually face all sorts of tests.

When I was living in Ireland once upon a time, I saw how my faith and commitment towards Islam could be tested.

If taqwa means to live life with full of caution like one who is traversing a path filled with thorns as defined by Ubay ibn Kaab (may Allah be pleased with him), then that taqwa is definitely needed when one is a resident in a country like Ireland.

Muslims can live as they wish in Ireland. They can eat or drink whatever they desire, mingle with anyone as they please and live a life without restrictions. Such a life however will take a toll on one's *IMAN* and ISLAM. Its destruction is upon the self and the future. Such are not the qualities of Muslims, *Mu'mins* or those who have *taqwa*. Those who have taqwa are the ones who are truly upon the guidance of Allah and will be victorious:

"Those are upon [right] guidance from their Lord, and it is those who are the successful." *(al-Baqarah 2:5)*

What Are We Actually Celebrating?

Every year when Ramadan is over, we celebrate *Eid al-Fitr.* We celebrate this festival with *TAKBIR*, *TASBIH* and *TAHMID*. But have we ever wondered, what is it are we actually celebrating?

Truly, that which we are celebrating is the fact that we are Muslims. We celebrate the greatest gift of Allah to us. Islam has ennobled us and preserved our dignity and humanity. That Islam, is the Islam that has been perfected by Allah, the Islam that symbolizes the perfection of Allah's favours upon us, and the Islam which He is pleased with as a way of life. We must praise Allah for this favour.

"Praise to Allāh, who has guided us to this; and we would never have been guided if Allāh had not guided us." *(Al-A'raf 7:43)*

Because of Islam, we are protected from being slaves of this world and materialism. Because of Islam too, we are saved from being slaves of our own *nafs*. And it is because of Islam we are free and liberated from being slaves to our fellow human beings. Islam helps us to stand with nobility even if we are a foreign minority *(ghuraba)* in the middle of others.

In fact, Islam makes us tough and resilient in the face of oppressive tribulations which seem to come from all directions. We have been oppressed with regards to human rights, our thoughts, our economic circumstance, socially, politically and in all other aspects of life. But have we ever felt the Islam inside us rotting away like wood eaten by termites? Never! If anything, these tribulations increase our certainty that they are part of the natural way of things that Allah has designed *(sunnatullah)* so he can reward those of us who manage to pull through.

We have never been apologetic about the laws and commands of Allah and in fact we are very firm and courageous in ennobling Islam, and worshipping Allah in the middle of a world full of tests and contradictions.

In his book 'At-thareeq ila al-quloon', Abbas As-Siesie writes that Hasan al-Banna inspired hope with the following words, "My dear brother, do not give up for giving up is not from the characteristics of the Muslims. The reality today was the dream yesterday, while the dream today will become the reality of tomorrow. The weak party won't be weak forever because the strong will slowly become old and feeble. Every being has his appointed time, and every oppression will come to an end."

So let us fill our celebration of *Eid al-Fitr* this time with a high spirit to strive and a passion to see the word of Allah prevail above all else. That is the key to success. Material achievement alone does not provide any guarantee of safety be it in this life or the next.

We should learn our lesson from the fall of Baghdad during the reign of the Abbasids. Those were the years when Muslims were at their peak of nonchalance towards the commands of Allah the Most High. So severe was their carelessness, Ibn Kathir (may Allah's mercy be upon him) narrates in his *al-Bidayah wa al-Nihayah* that in that year the Muslims in Baghdad forgot to pray the *Eid al-Fitr* prayer and made up for it after Maghrib! At that moment, when they could not care less about prayer, *da'wah*, enjoining good and forbidding evil, Allah destroyed them completely even though Baghdad was the center of civilization and knowledge of the world at the time.

Truly, in their story is a great lesson for those who ponder.

Allahu Akbar! Allahu Akbar! Allahu Akbar! Wa Lillahil Hamd!

Khutbah:
Self Liberation on *Eid al-Fitr*

The First *Khutbah*

Allahu Akbar, Allahu Akbar, Allahu Akbar, wa Lillahil Hamd.

Dear brothers and sisters *rahimakumullah*,

I remind myself and all of you to be mindful of the *TAQWA* generated in Ramadan, so it does not go to waste. Fear Allah as He should be feared and do not die except as Muslims.

Dear members of the congregation *rahimakumullah*,

Today is a day of festivities. A day that is filled with gratitude and joy, a day in which our Prophet (PBUH) forbade fasting. A day of celebration, a day to celebrate.

But what is the truth of what we are celebrating?

What is the reason for our happiness?

What is so significant about *Eid al-Fitr* that we are forbidden from fasting on this day?

These questions need to be contemplated upon or our joy is purposeless. One who is happy but does not know why he is happy is a mad man. One who is happy, but is happy for the wrong reason is actually in false happiness, in sorrow.

Our country Malaysia celebrates its greatest festival on the 31st of August. It is a day that is celebrated all over the country. What is so special about this day? It is none other than our Independence Day.

Man has the right to be happy when he is free and liberated. Free from imperialism and oppression, free from outside control, free from following the orders of others. This land is ours, so we have the right to reign over it, not anyone else.

Independence means return of the land to its owner, to its origin. If freedom from colonialism is the reason why 31st of August is so significant, what about the value behind the 1st of Shawwal? What is the reason for joy on *Eid al-Fitr?*

My dear Muslim brothers and sisters,

Do we still remember the purpose of Ramadan? Ramadan is given by Allah to us as a process in search of liberation.

All this while we have been ruled by two colonialists, both of whom are more difficult to face than the British, Japanese and Communist armies, or even any other force that we can see. The first colonialist is the devil. He is man's greatest enemy, constantly calling upon him to be disobedient to Allah as he promised God.

"*[Iblees]* said, "My Lord, because You have put me in error, I will surely make [disobedience] attractive to them [i.e., mankind] on earth, and I will mislead them all." *(Al-Hjir 15:39)*

Indeed, the one who is truly colonialized is he who cannot escape the calls of the devil in his life. A man who follows syaitan will move away from Allah little by little until his heart becomes blind to the truth.

Ramadan helps people escape the clutches of this first conqueror. The devil is chained to curb his potential and our veins are constricted via hunger so he cannot flow as easily.

On this first of Shawwal, we should ask ourselves, have we managed to release ourselves from the reigns of syaitan, from his enslavement? Have we succeeded in guarding our honor from being tainted due to the whispers of the accursed syaitan? Let us observe our daily actions and see how many of them are in line with the command of Allah and how many are in accordance with the whispers of syaitan?

If the devil no longer owns the 'remote control' of our lives, then we have a right to be joyful this Shawwal. Happy indeed are those who have freed themselves from the colonialism of syaitan and his government. As for those who have returned to heeding the call of syaitan after Ramadan, then call to mind these words of Allah:

[The hypocrites are] like the example of Satan when he says to man, "Disbelieve." But when he disbelieves, he says, "Indeed, I am disassociated from you. Indeed, I fear Allāh, Lord of the worlds." So the outcome for both of them is that they will be in the Fire, abiding eternally therein. And that is the recompense of the wrongdoers. *(Al-Hasyr 59:16-17)*

My dear Muslim brothers and sisters, may we be showered with Allah's mercy,

The second colonialist that controls man is the *nafs*. How many people out there live in free countries but are still slaves because they have no power to choose. They always follow the wants of this second colonialist, even if what it seeks is disastrous. Allah the Most High says:

"Have you seen he who has taken as his god his [own] desire, and Allāh has sent him astray due to knowledge and has set a seal upon his hearing and his heart and put over his vision a veil? So who will guide him after Allāh? Then will you not be reminded?" *(Al-Jathiyah 45:23)*

That is the greatest of colonialists.

Men conlonialised by their own selves, by their *nafs*, are not able to make their own decisions. They follow everything their *nafs* wants without question.

People who take their *nafs* as god are blind even if they have eyes that can see. They are deaf even if they have ears that can hear. They are foolish even if they may have a degree scroll. When man allows himself to be enslaved by his desires, his knowledge is no longer of any benefit. Having eyes that are blind, ears that are deaf and hearts which are sealed, are the consequences of obeying the *nafs* over God.

How many households are destroyed because men follow their *nafs*?

How many civilizations and governments were destroyed when their judgments were no longer centered on God, but on their desires?

All because man is not able to relinquish himself from his unlimited desires. The *nafs* yearns to swallow the whole earth even if it is only able to eat a plate.

Thus Allah gifts us Ramadan to educate us.

Do we remember, how we chose to abstain from eating despite having food all around us because we wanted to obey Allah? Do we remember, how we chose not to drink when there was water all around us because we wanted to obey Allah? Do we remember, how we lived as husband and wife but stayed away from conjugal relations during the day because we wanted to obey Allah?

All those are Ramadan's lessons in educating us to say NO to some of our wants so we learn good self-control. Have we managed to learn self-control and release ourselves from the grip of our *nafs*? Are we able to control our desires when it comes to evil things and remain rational when having to make decisions involving right and wrong?

If we have succeeded in liberating ourselves from the enslavement of our *nafs*, then we have a right to be joyful for we have truly succeeded. Allah says:

"And [by] the soul and He who proportioned it And inspired it [with discernment of] its wickedness and its righteousness, He has succeeded who purifies it, And he has failed who instills it [with corruption]." *(Ash-Shams 91:7-10)*

Liberation from the enslavement of *shaitan* and our *nafs* is indeed a true liberation that is celebrated during *Eid al-Fitr,* that is the return of man to his original state, the *Fitrah*.

My dear Muslim brothers and sisters, *rahimakumullah,*

Eid al-Fitr and *Eid al-Adha* are our festivals. They are both endorsed by the Prophet (PBUH) as festivals for the Muslims.

Anas says: "The Messenger of Allah *(sal Allahu alaihi wa sallam)* came to Madinah and the people had two days when they would play and have fun. He said, 'What are these two days?' They said, 'We used to play and have fun on these days during the Jaahiliyyah (Days of Ignorance). The Messenger of Allah *(sal Allahu alaihi wa sallam)* said, 'Allah has given you something better than them, the day of *(Eid) Adhaa* and the day of *(Eid) Fitr.'" [Sunan Abu Dawood - Classed as Sahih by Shaykh al-Albaani]*

We have been given *Eid al-Fitr* so we become unique and special. We are not Jews nor Christians. We are different and so are our celebrations.

Therefore, we must enliven our *Eid* our way, the Islamic way which is pleasing to Allah, and not the way of the devil, the *nafs,* or the Jews and Christians.

We are allowed to enjoy some entertainment. In fact the Prophet (PBUH) reprimanded Abu Bakr al-Siddiq (may Allah be pleased with him) when he rebuked two girls who sang during the *Eid* by saying, "O Abu Bakr! There is an *Eid* for every nation and this is our *Eid.*" *[Bukhari]*

Today is the day for us to be entertained and be happy.

But do not let our excessive entertainment prove once again that we are a people without dignity, without identity, who have failed to free ourselves from the Jewish and Christian form of entertainment called HEDONISME.

Man's addiction to the entertainment drug called hedonism is very terrifying. He knows the dangers of hedonism, but because of his addiction to it he refuses to repent and instead quickly returns to consume this excessive form of entertainment right after Ramadan on the morning of *Eid al-Fitr*.

Stay away from this drug. Call to mind the advice of the Prophet (PBUH):

Abu Sa'eed al-Khudri (may Allah be pleased with him) narrated that the Prophet (peace and blessings of Allah be upon him) said: "You will certainly follow the ways of those who came before you hand span by hand span, cubit by cubit, to the extent that if they entered the hole of a lizard, you will enter it too." We said: "O Messenger of *Allah*, (do you mean) the Jews and the Christians?" He said: "Who else?" *(Narrated by al-Bukhaari, 1397; Muslim, 4822)*

Allahu Akbar! Allahu Akbar! Allahu Akbar! Laa Ilaaha Illa Allah! Allahu Akbar wa lillahil hamd!

The Second *Khutbah*

Dear Muslims,

Now that Ramadan is over, defend the success that we have achieved. Do not let the mosques become empty. The obligatory prayers have more right to be done in congregation than *v*. Do not forget to fast optionally for six days in Shawwal as well as on other days when it is recommended to fast. Orphans should not be left as orphans for the remaining 11 months. Acts of worship and welfare must be continued.

Indeed, the length of our death is longer than the length of our life. Hence, we should work hard in this life so we can rest well upon death. Do not rest too much now lest we suffer in death!

On the authority of Abi Amr – and it also said Abi Amrah – Sufyan ibn Abdillah (may Allah be pleased with him) who said: "I said, "O Messenger of Allah, tell me a statement about Islam such that I will not have to ask anyone other than you". He answered, "Say, I believe in Allah and then stand firm and steadfast to that". *[Muslim]*

Hoping for Forgiveness

"*Allahu Akbar....Allahu Akbar....*" The Imam began his sermon. His voice was full of energy.

At that moment, I was stroking the hair of Saiful Islam who was leaning on my lap after the *Eid* prayer.

My feelings were mixed. There was a lot on my mind.

During the last two to three days of Ramadan, I was so anxious thinking about having to bid farewell to it. I could not appreciate the joy of *Eid al-Fitr* and instead felt guilty towards my children, afraid that this anxiety would affect their happiness in celebrating the *Eid*. The children are innocent, and so as a father, if I am not able to be happy, I need to muster the strength to make them happy because it is their right.

Moreover, Saiful Islam managed to fast 20 full days on his first attempt.

The atmosphere of the sermon was tranquil after the mild drizzle on the Fajr of the 1st of Shawwal.

Seeking Forgiveness: Culture or Act of Worship

After the sermon, I stood up and shook hands with the people around me. There was something amiss about how people said, *"Selamat Hari Raya, maaf zahir batin"* (literally Happy Festival Day, forgiveness from within and without).

"There are no two Muslims who meet and shake hands with one another, but they will be forgiven before they part." *Narrated by Abu Dawood (5212)*

But is the forgiveness really sincere, or is it just a cultural phrase that is uttered without any meaning? Can the hearts of two people shaking hands be attuned to one another if the phrase declared is empty and void of any meaning or feeling? Can such empty words bring about the forgiveness promised by Him?

Of all the prayers uttered by all those shaking hands, I do not wish for this one prayer to come from a heedless heart. I must mean it. I must really feel it. My heart yearns for the forgiveness from my mother..... a forgiveness that is not mere 'decoration' for the *Eid*, but a true seeking of forgiveness that will determine whether I can attain peace or not.

I quickly began looking for mother.

Forgive Your Son

"Mother, I ask for your forgiveness. I hardly come home to the village to see you and call only once in a while. You are lonely at home. Forgive me mother!" I kissed her hand and hugged her.

Mother's old and thin body shivered. She cried too, voiceless. Only her sobs could be heard.

I did not want to delay anymore. Everything had to be purified that morning. I wanted to be reborn like a clean white cloth. Only the forgiveness of Allah and then of my mother could make that possible.

"I really really seek your forgiveness, mother," I continued to hug mother tightly.

"Yes... me too.... I am old..... I...." How difficult it was for mother to finish her words.

In my mother's embrace, it felt as if tranquility had descended from the sky.... It was like being hugged by the heavens.

But that is mother. The one who is at fault is me, the child, but mother is always like that, never tired of forgiving. Such magnanimity can only come from the heart of a mother who loves her children with an UNCONDITIONAL LOVE. In fact, in the midst of forgiving, she asked for forgiveness herself.

Forgiveness That Results in Greater Love

People may be able to forgive, but rarely will that forgiveness lead to more love. The tongue may utter forgiveness, but the heart resists another meeting. People forgive because they want all matters to be sorted here. "I don't wish to see you in the Hereafter!" the heart says after a bitter forgiveness that may not mend a broken friendship.

The same though cannot be said of Allah, Al-Ghafoor, Al-Raheem. Not only is He Oft-forgiving, but also Most Merciful and Loving. Not only does He love to forgive, but every person who seeks forgiveness is loved by Him. Forgiveness followed by His love is something sublime. That is He, Allah who is Ghaffar, Allah who is Raheem.

There is none amongst the creation that is able to follow that mould .... To forgive, and then to love. In fact, the more someone has to forgive another, the bitterer their relationship becomes, except in the case of mothers.

It is only mothers that Allah has gifted with such a tendency. Children who seek forgiveness are forgiven unconditionally because of their love, and the more we ask for forgiveness from our mothers, the greater their love for us. The heart of a mother.....

My mother is old. Her age is like the evening is to the rest to the day, and I do not want to leave her alone and sad anymore. My heart cannot bear the burden of regret every time I imagine her eating rice alone on the table that was once full of fun and laughter of the whole family.

I hope my lips will always be wet from constant prayer for you.

And I hope I will always make time to speak and listen to you, dear mother.

"And lower to them the wing of humility out of mercy and say, "My Lord, have mercy upon them as they brought me up [when I was] small."" *(al-Isra' 17:24)*

That Evening

"That story holds a great meaning for me," brother Zabidi Mohamed said.

I stared dreamily into space, beholding the red glow of sunset. My companion, al-Adib by my side, was quiet too.

That evening I took the opportunity to accompany al-Adib to meet brother Zabidi Mohamed, a unique and prolific scriptwriter. We spoke about many things, including new ideas about how to produce dramas of higher quality.

"What or who do you think is the main actor in the drama Ihsan?" Zabidi asked.

"Maybe most would say Nordin. As for me, I think the main actor is Zamri, the magistrate. The weight of the story lies on Zamri. A good son, but unconsciously sinful because he was so BUSY. A BUSYNESS that became the cause for his mother's LONELINESS and SADNESS," I said.

My eyes felt hot from tears that began to flow.

We fell silent.

The discussion that evening was solemn.

Not Alqamah

Many would be reminded of the story of Alqamah.

The story of Alqamah is narrated by Imam adh-Dhahabi (may Allah have mercy on him) in his book *al-Kabaair* while Ibn Hajar al-Haitami collected in his *az-Zawwajir*. In both books, the narration is attributed to at-Tabarani and Ahmad without any commentary on the chain of narration or any verdict on the authenticity of the narration. That said, Shaykh al-Albani in his commentary on the book *Al-targheeb wa al-Tarheeb* by Imam al-Hafeedz al-Mundhiri mentions that the story of Alqamah is extremely weak.

The famous story of Alqamah which may have been an inspiration to the drama Ihsan, (which tells the story of a treacherous child), is different to my situation. Different in that the reality of how much I wished for mother's forgiveness was because of the pain and anxiety of my spirit due to my carelessness, which felt like a fire in a wound. If something is not right, do not delay. We must quickly rectify the wrongs we have committed against our mothers.

May the forgiveness I sought from mother yesterday morning be a provision that will light up the path of *Mardhatillah* until I achieve *Husnul Khatimah*. Ameen ya Allah!

The Sign of Love in Shawwal

"Bedah, dad and mum are going to the mosque. If it rains, please bring in the clothes on the clothes line. Don't forget *ok!*" Haji Ahmad shouted from his car. Bedah nodded, smiling while locking the gates.

Thunder could be heard in the skies, the sign of heavy clouds waiting to pour.

Right after the Dhuhr prayer and talk, Haji Ahmad and his wife drove home.

"Hopefully Bedah did not forget about the clothes. The rain earlier was so heavy, it was difficult to even hear what the speaker was saying!" Hajah Asma said to her husband. Haji Ahmad nodded in agreement.

When they arrived home, they were relieved to see no clothes on the clothes line. Bedah is such a dependable child!

When they walked into the house, their relief turned to happiness. Grateful and touched.

Bedah not only brought the clothes in, but she had ironed them, folded them and kept them nicely in the cupdboards!

Do you think Haji Ahmad and Hajah Asma would love a daughter like Bedah? She was only told to take the clothes in if it rains and just leave it in on the sofa. But this young girl did more than what she was asked.

Of course they would love her!

The optional acts are a sign of love which invites more love!

My invitation to the dear readership of this book is that let us fast 6 days in Shawwal. Allah obligated upon us the fast of Ramadan, but we should do a little extra as a sign of our love for Him. As I mentioned before, the 6-day fast of Shawwal is like the *rawatib* of the obligatory prayers.

Indeed, the fast of Ramadan is a sign of our obedience to Him. Let the fast of Shawwal be the sign of our love for Him.

Abu Ayyub (may Allah be pleased with him) reported that the Messenger of Allah (peace be upon him) said: "Whoever fasts Ramadan and follows it with six days of Shawwal, it will be as if he fasted for a lifetime." *Narrated by Muslim, Abu Dawud, At-Tirmidhi, An-Nisa'i and Ibn Majah.*

About the Author

HASRIZAL ABDUL JAMIL

Hasrizal holds a Bachelor of Sharia (Honours) from Mu'tah University, Jordan (2001). He is the academic director at Khalifah Model School (Secondary), an integrated private Islamic school owned by Khalifah Education Foundation. Currently on his study leave in education at the University of Oulu Finland. A strong believer in progressive curriculum and instruction, welcoming technology-enhanced learning to support pedagogical needs. Area of interest includes regulations of metacognition and motivation in learning, with emphasis on Islamic education.

Hasrizal succeeded in bookwriting after his *AKU TERIMA NIKAHNYA (2008)* became one of the National Best Sellers. He proceeded with many more books, such as *BERCINTA SAMPAI KE SYURGA (2009)*, *MURABBI CINTA (2010)*, *RINDU BAU POHON TIN (2009)*, *SECANGKIR TEH PENGUBAT LETIH (2010)*, *TRANSFORMASI RAMADAN (2011)*, *EDISI*

ISTIMEWA AKU TERIMA NIKAHNYA – *Trilogy (2012)*, *DI HAMPARAN SHAMROCK KUSERU NAMA-MU (2012)*, *ERTI HIDUP PADA MEMBERI (2013)*, and the most recent, *TAK KENAL MAKA TAK CINTA (2014)*, *MENALAR MAKNA DIRI: KEMBARA MENJEJAK IMAM BIRGIVI (2014)*, and *SETIA DENGAN KEBENARAN (2017)*.

AQTAR MOHAMED UMMAR

Aqtar Mohamed Ummar graduated from the University of Edinburgh with a medical degree in 2012. After working as a doctor for a very short time, he resigned and decided to pursue his passion in teaching. He taught in two government schools for about a year and half as a substitute teacher before pursuing a master's degree in Integrative Neuroscience at Edinburgh University also. Upon return from Edinburgh, he was offered a job as Chemistry and Biology teacher at KMSS. Currently, he is Head of Academic Division and teaches *Islamiyyat* and Biology at IGCSE level, apart from being a tutor for the tahfiz program.

Made in the USA
Monee, IL
23 April 2020